No ocd

One Family's Journey Through Obsessive Compulsive Disorder

Frederique

iUniverse, Inc.
Bloomington

No ocd
One Family's Journey Through Obsessive-Compulsive Disorder

iUniverse books may be ordered through booksellers or by contacting:

iUniverse
1663 Liberty Drive
Bloomington, IN 47403
www.iuniverse.com
1-800-Authors (1-800-288-4677)

ISBN: 978-1-4620-3854-1 (sc)
ISBN: 978-1-4620-3855-8 (e)

Printed in the United States of America

iUniverse rev. date: 12/20/2011

Dedication

To : Everyone who has ever felt anxious.

Thanks and Acknowledgments:

As I progress on my journey, my heart is filled with gratitude and innumerable feelings of appreciation to so many people.

I would like to begin by thanking God for giving me the strength to face my fears and for giving to me the wonderful people that I have in my life.

I would like to thank now my wonderful parents. I really cannot express all of my thanks to you here. When I look back to where I was and still can be at times with my ocd, I feel disgraceful, not so much because I put myself through all of that, but I now see that I dragged you, my parents, through the muck and mire of ocd with me, too. Can I apologize enough? I would not have gotten this far without your love and support for me.

Dad, thank you for working on your ocd and helping me with mine. I know that when no one else "gets" the ocd stuff, that you will. You have helped me, and I appreciate not just your help, but you, more than you know.

Mom, thank you so much for all of your patience with me. I never expected that you could or should make it all better. I wish you could know that you've helped me ever so much with all of your reassurance and helping me to see things from a non-ocd point of view, and that is ever so helpful for me when my "reality check bounces". Thanks for holding my hands and continuing to help me.

Stephanie, Chuck and Sarah, Elaine, Michelle and Joe, The entire "Shiver" troupe, Angela, Ron, "Moose" and Sharon, and those of you who don't want your names printed here… my dear true friends, you laugh with me and not at me. You are there for me and I'm there for you, too. You guys rock. Or Raq. You know who you are.

A big thank you to the people who so kindly helped me with proofreading, the press and general ideas and support. Frank, Jeff Bell, John B., Mark S., Sandra and Lynnette, Jackie, Stephanie, Steve, John, Peter and Michael, you have my appreciation.

I say we all get together and have a big group hug now.

Introduction

Psssst…

Are you like me?

If you are you probably skip the introduction to most books. However, I ask that you please read this one. I'll make it brief, I promise, but I'm explaining where I'm coming from and I think it'll enhance your experience with this book. Thank you!

Yes, no, yes, no, yes, no, yes.

That's how my inner dialogue spoke to me when I thought on starting to write tonight.

Had I thought something disrespectful to God? I prayed about it. I asked forgiveness. One of my next thoughts was should I skip writing all together. Why should I not write at all? How does that tie in to a thought I had earlier? It all sounds illogical, I'm certain. You can admit it. Right now you're probably thinking about how illogical and possibly crazy that line of reasoning sounds. You know why I say that? Because I think it's illogical and crazy sounding when I type it, and yet I'm the person who has the fear! As irrational as it seems, this same reasoning is how my ocd has managed to keep me under its thumb for most of the years of my life. It's how I've managed to wash my hands until I'm bleeding, and how I've quite effectively written myself out of my own life at times. Writing yourself out of your own life is a lot easier than it sounds. It begins with the same fear I mentioned above. "Punishing" yourself for thoughts you've had. It's something that I will talk about further in the coming chapters, along with how to wash your hands bloody, clean remotes with soap and running water, clean phones with bleach, and I want to even share some of my most humiliating fears. Why would I want to do this? I have obsessive compulsive disorder, quite severe. I was diagnosed at age fourteen, but have had symptoms since I was a child. I feel ocd gets misrepresented quite a bit. In my opinion, everyone has a little bitty bit of ocd tendencies. That's why some people casually brush it off. But severe ocd is nothing to brush off. It's tormenting, and robs the person experiencing it of time, energy and happiness. On the other hand, people with ocd aren't "crazy" nor do they suffer from retardation. Granted retardation is a real condition and is not mentioned in any disrespectful manner here. But it isn't the same as ocd. I want to write this book based on my very own experiences with the disorder. I want to entertain. Go ahead and laugh with me, but please not at me. I also aim to enlighten. I would like people who don't have ocd to understand it better. I would like people with it to know that they're not alone, and last but not least, I would like to share what has worked to lessen my symptoms.

Why isn't ocd capitalized? It's an abbreviation, I know. But I refuse to put it in high case letters. It doesn't deserve it.

About the Title of This Book, or, What is "nocd"?

"Nocd" was a beautiful thought I had one day. My cd player, in its small digital display, flashes a similar message when you try to play a cd, but there is none to be played. At first glance, it could look like ocd. Until you notice the "n". "No cd". " Nocd". "Noocd". "No ocd". And what a message it is. What would life be like without this brain-drain called ocd? It's a question I, and I'm sure many other ocd "experiencers" as I like to call them, simply cannot fathom. I am not giving up the fight to wellness even though it has been a huge fight for most of my life. I am not letting this boogey man of mental disorders live my life for me, and I hope to turn this incredibly negative thing, into something positive.

Earliest ocd Memories

Whooooosh! The water filled the sink, and the soap I had put in made bubbles so big it almost overflowed. I finally shut off the water. It was a stretch but I made it. Did I mention I was three years old and standing on a step stool at my grandma's apartment? I was washing Mary and Jospeh from a Nativity set. But not Baby Jesus. I'm not sure where the baby Jesus from that set is. It's been years since I've seen that Mary and Joseph, but I still remember them plain as can be. Plaster or a similar material, dressed in beautiful gold painted clothing, faces painted fleshtones and hair painted dark. The first time I washed them they were dirty. Well, probably not dirty in any conventional sense, but dusty and household grit in minute details of their draped clothing. I felt so good, like I was doing something nice. Seeing them clean when I got done made me feel good. I liked the very essence of doing that. Filling the sink with warm water that felt nice on my hands and arms. The pretty bubbles the soap made made my eyes delight. The scent of the soap that smelled like flowers. I loved it, especially the part when I was done, seeing them all shiny and clean. I started doing it each time I was there. So much that the painted started chipping off. The adults didn't think it was too odd. Something a little kid might do. Kind of cute. Even though I was only three at the time, I still remember it. I believe it was the beginning of my ocd problem. As I grew a few years older, I heard adults tell stories of assorted illnesses. Blood poisining stuck out to me. Cut yourself on rusty wire and apparently a red line would go to your heart. I worried about most of the little cuts and scrapes I used to get from playing outside. Had I cut myself on something rusty? Was that a red line starting on its way to my heart? I did a lot of asking. I remember it bothered me more at night. Other than that, I don't remember my ocd causing me much of a problem. As I grew older, I even enjoyed reading books like "The Hot Zone" by Michael Crichton. That was bound to change. I became a pre-teen and then teenager.

Teenage Wonderland

As a pre-teen, I had wondered about this teenager business. The way some people talked about it, it seemed like this fantastic adventure where everything would come together and make sense. Come to think on it, that was how popular culture and some movies had portrayed it as well.

Cough, cough…. Hack, snort. I blew my nose, again. No, I wasn't suffering from anything rare. I was 13 and had a head cold. I'm sure that almost no one likes being sick, but I really didn't like it. What I hated in particular was when my ear or ears stuffed up. I hated how it felt, and how it sounded. My own voice sounded strange and anything else too, like brushing my teeth, made me aware of the pressure in my head. I was secretly, or not so secretly, worried that I was going to go deaf. I tried to get my ears to snap and drain. It didn't always work. I'd panic. I'd ask my dad and my mom over and over again. "Am I going to go deaf?" "Am I going to get better?" "When will I get better?", and then let's not forget the minute details I'd get into. Stuff like, "I've been sick for this many days, and I'm still sick, does that mean my ears will stay stuffy?" … what if, what if, what if. More and more detailed questions. They'd get frustrated at me. Looking back, I don't blame them. But at the time, I couldn't figure out why they weren't as worried about it as I was. I was reassured that colds only last so long. But it didn't seem to matter to me. I'd get more nervous the longer the cold stretched on. To me at the time, it seemed to signify that I was going to stay stuck in a cold-like state. Back then we didn't have any form of health insurance whatsoever. Supposing we did, I'd have likely been pestering some patient doctor weekly. So it became another thing I'd ask endless questions about. "If I get this – or – that symptom, can I go to the doctor?" "If this-or-that symptom doesn't clear up, can I go to the doctor?" Usually the answer was yes, but I was told it probably wasn't going to be needed, at which my anxiety would rise. I would like to stress right here and now that I wasn't suffering from anything other at the time than sinus infections or common cold. But it felt serious to me. I can't begin to guess how much of my time the cold fear would take up. In addition to simply asking questions, I'd give constant updates about the minute details of my health. "I blew my nose twice, and the first time my ears cracked, but the second time they didn't." or "I felt like I had to sneeze, but I coughed instead". At the time, I didn't see it as being boring or selfish, but as I look back, that's entirely what it must have come across as. Deep down I was looking for reassurance that I would get well. Now that's not a bad thing, but needing reassurance 24/7 is another issue altogether. It's stressful, both for the seekers and for the givers. As seemingly traumatic as my getting sick was for me, as soon as I started to mend the anxiety would lessen up. Whew. It was like a weight had been lifted off of my shoulders. But the ocd needed something to keep me worried about.

Overactive Self Proctection

After I had gotten well, my thoughts shifted from getting well to keeping well. Over the years, this has been a consistant theme of my ocd, with the feared illness changing. It began simple enough. From my previous example, I was afraid of getting the common cold. At the time, I wrote letters to pen pals and I had about 80 of them worldwide. I remember getting one envelope in the mail. It had a odd black smudge on it. That smudge stayed with me in my thoughts night and day. What was it? What could it be? In all likelyhood, it was a chunk off of one of my first eyeliner pencils, because the letter had been laying near it. But in my over active ocd mindset, it could have been that, sure. Or it could have been grease from the mail sorting machines. Or it could have been a dangerous virus released into the mail system that just managed to adhere itself to one of my letters. I freaked out. I asked tons of questions about it. I washed my hands nearly contantly. This was back when I still would use bar soap. Contaminated object. And... Funny thing was, I washed a lot, until my hands would chap. But I still didn't "feel clean". My hands felt a physical sensation of being dirty. I started my theory of contamination by a contaminated object. After that came my theory of contamination of contamination by a ... - you can imagine where it went from there. The letter had touched the desk, the pen had touched the spot where the letter was and was now on the floor. I had maybe stepped on the spot on the floor and tracked letter-pen-desk-floor germs all over the floor. The floor became something to be avoided. I don't remember how I cleaned things in those days. I really did realize that whatever was on that letter was probably safe. But that "what if" was too risky in my mind. My mind went into overdrive. I imagined scenes where I had contracted black smudge disease from the envelope. What the doctor would say to me. What if I had infected other people? What if it was an unknown and incurable disease? Other things got to me too. Letters no longer had to have mysterious marks on them. They could be sent from a sender who had the common cold. Going out in public became difficult. People would cough, sneeze or otherwise look at me strange, and I thought they had some kind of catchable. I held my breath. I held my hands in a just-so way on my lap until I could wash them. And wash I did. I can't begin to guess how many times. The sink would fill up with soap scum. My hands would dry out, and then crack and bleed. And I would get even more paranoid. Blood meant an open door for germs to get in. I would wash and band-aid. The band-aid ritual would be come intense. My hands had to be clean to touch the band aid. And the band aid had to touch only clean things. I don't know how many band aids I threw away unused. Finally I would get it on, and then it wouldn't last because I would still be washing. I started washing higher up on my wrists and then finally my arms. After my dad told me my hands looked like an 80 year olds, my parents recommended me to use butter, because at this time even a lot of the most gentle lotions burned like fire on my raw skin. Butter felt good though. But I didn't let it stay long enough to really heal my hands.

The People Pleaser

When I was a kid, I remember trying to be fair. And then I remember getting really, really angry when the "favor" wasn't returned to me. As I grew older this became a dangerous habit. My personality type dreads arguments and controversy. So I became a grand genius at being a sell out. This-or-that new friend simply loves something. Doesn't matter what really, a band, a movie, an actor, politics or any other array of things. Things I didn't really enjoy, appreciate or whatever. And even disagreeing on simple matters like these was difficult for me. So, sometimes I would cheesily go along to get along. Of course, outright lying bothered, and still does, bother me, so I would think of inventive ways to get around answering with something that was contrary to what someone else thought.

I think what drives my people pleasing is fear of rejection. Fear that having my own opinion will turn people against me. Fear that by speaking my mind I will turn into the arrogant ignoramuses that I'm sure so many of us encounter and dislike.

I did, and still do, favors and more favors. Favors that cost me money and favors that eat into my time. Favors that make me resent myself. A recent example is when I was sitting with a friend who had just been let out of surgery. I dropped her off, picked her up and sat with her for most of the afternoon, until: 1.) I had to leave for night school, and 2.) she had another friend coming over. As someone with low blood sugar, I enjoy eating on time, and especially so I can stay awake for four hour classes. I had figured in just enough time to grab a bite to eat and then go to school. As I was leaving, the chance to stick up for myself presented itself. She asked if I could get her a soda. I usually get mixed up in this part of town, and besides, I had figured just enough time to grab a bite and get to school on time. I hesitated answering. I paused and a long awkward silence drew out. Thoughts whisked through my head. "I have just enough time to grab some food and get to school." "She has another friend coming over, why can't she just call her friend and have her bring it?" "Why is her time more valuable than mine?" Of course, the thought that won out was "She's your friend and just got out of surgery. Wouldn't you want someone to do it for you?" I said sure. And I kicked myself. Naturally, I got confused on my way back to her place, but I did come through. And you know what? In spite of myself, I started to resent this friend. I feel that she's better than me. And then I resent myself for resenting her. The only reason I feel that she's better than me is because I have put myself at the bottom of the list. My resentment is my own fault.

And, if I don't watch it, I'll eventually blow up, which is probably just the steam that is building up in me from days, weeks and possibly years of holding back.

I even realize that people love people who are themselves. Who are true, real and genuine. Who speak their minds. People don't much like those who are quiet and word things in tricky ways in order to not offend. I'm learning slowly but surely.

Recently I told someone my real, honest opinion even though it differed from theirs. And it went fine. Being untrue to yourself is not fair to you, and it isn't even fair to anyone else either.

An Unpopular, Popular Girl

Taking a brief break from the ocd, I grew up in the beautiful countryside of west central Minnesota. It was fabulously pretty. I could go outside and have mini-adventures. I would walk through my own paths and enjoy the outdoors. It was like living in a national park. My parents and I did not fit in. The rest of the community was Norwegian and mostly related. They knew practically everyone. They were related to practically everyone. They didn't take kindly to stranger Germans moving in for the most part. After their curiosity was satisfied, then you were pretty much left on your own. They would tolerate people who did business with them. But not much else. Cliquey would be the best word to describe it.

I was homeschooled and cannot begin to say how happy I am that I was. I can't imagine what some of those children would have been like. Of course, living in a cliquey community and being homeschooled didn't give me a lot of friends. It bothered me. It seemed like other girls my age were having sleepovers and going to the mall. Stuff I wanted to do. Don't get me wrong, we tried 4-H. I did well and enjoyed doing projects, but I didn't make friends with the other kids there. They would talk to me and all, but they didn't go out of their way to be friendly.

I tried calling some of them. I got told that they weren't allowed to talk on the phone. I wasn't the most socially adept person ever, but that seemed a little farfetched to me. I would make acquaintances. Later on, I realized one girl probably had a crush on my dad. "*I want to go talk to your parents. Your dad's so smart. *giggle**". Duh. Some tried to get me to sell their shop-from-home products. Homeschool groups weren't yet popular. I was shy and didn't really know how to behave in front of other people. I still don't. But I can act to some extent.

One childhood friend grew far different from me. I had trouble adapting to it. I was taking walks outside, playing with dolls and reading books. She was into boys, looking hot, and possibly some other stuff that I won't list here. To her, I was probably this geeky drag to be around. And to me, well, I just plain out didn't know why she was making jokes at my expense.

So, with all that, you're probably wondering where the "popular" part comes in? Like I say, I had around 80 pen pals. Some of them I still have today. I seemed to be someone people liked advice from. I still am today. With the advent of the internet, I grew even more popular online on some select message boards. Of course, then came love... but that's another section.

Madness

I'm not sure how or when it happened, but the fear of colds turned into the fear of rabies. I was still a teen. Likely fourteen or so. I remember watching the sad movie "Old Yeller" as a child. Maybe that's what started it. I don't know. Pretty soon things outside became dirty and I no longer enjoyed going on my mini outdoor adventures. A rabid animal might have spat on the ground, which I would carry in on my shoes, which, if it got into any cut, could make me have rabies. In my mind at least. Even sitting on the deck after sunset, something I used to like, became tricky. In the country, the bats would fly around and eat mosquitoes. I'd wince when they'd fly overhead. "*They won't fly into you*", I was told. But it wasn't that I was afraid of. I was afraid they'd spit on me. So after dark became time for Frederique to go inside.

After I'd started taking music lessons, my parents and I were driving home. As a special treat, we were going out to eat. We stepped out of the car, and it was after dark. I saw a shadowy thing above head. Sure enough. One of the evil shadow creatures. A bat. I really freaked out that time. When we got in the restaurant, I washed so many times in the bathroom. I can remember washing the top of my head and my hair. I remember washing my hands again and again because I had touched something. I remember rubbing soap into my clothing. It was exhausting. I launched an extensive line of questioning. To be sure, I even asked if you could get rabies from tongue kissing a bat. Don't ask me how asking that question alleviated my fears, but it did. I could finally settle down. For a little while.

We got home and I recall being concerned about my paper sheets that the guitar lessons were written on. I wanted to keep my guitar teacher safe, too. So I grabbed the bleach bottle and put a dot or two along with water on a rag and wiped off my papers. Surprisingly, bleach won't take ink out if it's used in that small of proportions. It will make paper curl up funny though.

Years later, I would walk past a bat on the ground at a newly paved parking lot and freak out. I didn't step on or near the bat, but it worried me, as did the shoes I wore. In those days, I would even avoid certain words like "wild". For some reason I related it to rabies and wild animals. I would like to say that the rabies fear is over, but I have had bouts of the rabies fear as recently as 2009 when my mom and I reencountered the shoes I had worn six years ago in that parking lot. I still consider that spot in my closet contaminated.

Also, in 2009, I noticed two little close together scabs on my chest. I didn't remember getting them. The exact place where they were they really might have been anything. Pimples, scuff marks from getting dressed or even cat claw marks from picking up my kitty, Josie. Of course, my ocd mindset went straight to worst case, and I wondered if I had been bitten by a rabid animal, even though there was no real evidence to support it. I panicked and even had a bad dream about a bat that I couldn't get away from. It all goes to show that even when you think one fear is conquered, it can be right there, under the surface.

Ebola Fear

As I mentioned earlier, before I was afriad of germs, I actually read books like Michael Crichton's "The Hot Zone", a book about the ebola virus. With all of its gory details, I should have figured that this would be fertile ground for the seeds of ocd.

Sometime after the common cold fear, I became afriad of ebola. Mostly in mysterious marks on things. The book page has an abnormally dark spot. I don't remember that stain being on my clothing. Maybe it was the ebola virus. My fears would kick into gear.

And when I'd get a headache, which was rare for me, I'd really worry. In the book, that was among the first symptoms for the ebola virus. And because I didn't get headaches often, I'd really wonder about it.

But the strangest thing the ebola fear had me do was throw away a shirt. We had gone to a beautiful park in the area. This park had port-a-potties. As you can guess, I pretty well dislike the whole port-a-pot idea. But sometimes you have little or no choice. After I went in, I saw a plastic baggie on the floor, and the ring was wet. I freaked out. What if a scientist had been there, someone who'd worked in a lab with the ebola virus.

He'd smuggled it out of there in a plastic bag, to use for who knows what purpose, and then decided to dump it right in a port-a-pot. What if that liquid was the ebola virus. My rational mind told me that this long, made up story just wasn't at all likely. But, yet again, the "what if" and all the gory details I'd read were almost too much for me to contend with.

That trip to the park that should have been fun, became a torment. All I could think about was how to clean myself. We finally went to town. I used the bathroom and washed for what felt like hundreds of times. I used scads of those brown paper towels. I tried to throw them in the small garbage can. It overflowed onto the floor. The sink looked like Niagara Falls if someone would have thrown thousands of gallons of soap into it. Watery and bubbley. I made a real mess in that bathroom. I finally left in my still contaminated clothing.

When I would return to that grocery store and that bathroom in the future, I would see a sarcastic note by the paper towels. Something to the effect of, "You only need one towel. Not 100!", in angry thick writing. I felt a little angry at the person not only for not understanding that I, by washing and using close to 100 towels, could have saved the world from an outbreak, but for not understanding that some people are scared of germs. On the other hand, I knew that they probably didn't think of any of that.

What a foreign concept to me. They probably were the ones that had to clean up my Niagara-sink mess. In a way, it made me feel famous, too. At least someone had noticed what I had done.

I still had to contend with my clothing, though. I must have washed things I came into contact with, too, but at this point I really don't remember that. I remember being more afraid of the shirt I was wearing that day. Even though it had been washed, and in theory was as clean as everything else that I kept and wore out of the load of laundry it was in, it still felt very dirty. I threw it in a far corner of the closet. I waited and waited. It got in the way. It contaminated other things. I tossed it.

Thankfully the ebola fear left, eventually. But it was likely to be replaced by some other germ- related fear.

The funny thing about my germ fear is: the symptoms remain the same. The dreadful imagination. The fear of something incurable. The fear of getting people who I love sick. But the feared disease changes. There is always something new to get used to. Once one fear is conquered, the ocd needs to keep scaring me, and doubtless many others, into its submission.

AIDS Fear

In my teen years I didn't date much. I certainly didn't have sex. One needs a partner to do that. With my fear of blood, getting cut and needles, I certainly didn't do injectible street drugs. And with my fear of pills and other substances, I didn't do other non-injectible street drugs either. But I would still worry about AIDS.

I would layer public toilet seats with toilet paper to fit between me and the seat, when they didn't provide the toilet seat gaskets you find in some public restrooms. I would worry about catching aids off of plates, forks, spoons and/or napkins.

I saw my first real life gay people when I was a teen. At least I highly suspect they were gay. They were on a date at the China Buffet. I stared. I, myself, feel that it isn't a spiritually right lifestyle. That's why I'm not gay. However, I don't judge others if they are. I have some gay friends who are dear friends of mine.

But with AIDS and its connection to the gay community, I began imagining gay people. I was at a store once and a man was coughing. He might have been gay. I felt something on the back of my neck. Could it have been a fine mist of his saliva from coughing? What if this maybe gay guy had coughed on me? Did I have aids?

Of course, I realized that not all gay people have AIDS. But the what if was way too big. Yet again, as with a lot of my previous fears and the ocd imagination, I'd get huge welts and grow thin. Now I had wanted to be thin, but I didn't want to be thin in that scary of a way. I'd slowly sink into a lethargic state as my immune system caved in to the secondary infections. I wouldn't date anyone, because if I had aids, that wouldn't be too nice of me to spread it to anyone else. I might give it to my parents. I might give it to other people in the same way that this maybe gay guy had possibly given it to me by coughing on me. As with the pregnancy fear, people would think it was unheard of. Girl gets aids from coughing man. Unlikely. People would think I was a slut.

I washed and washed and washed. I washed my hands, wrists, arms and face, and threw my clothes in the the hamper. I streaked soap through my hair and attempted to rinse it out by the sink. I even remember the soap, it was a special kind of citrus liquid soap. And I was using it up quite fast. I washed my purchases from said store. I asked numerous questions.

Eventually the aids fear subsided. The American Red Cross website helped with that. As it turns out, you can't get aids from anything other than sexual exchanges and blood. So my contaminated chair theory was out.

But at the time, as with so many other fears, the ocd-imagination and the what if story were way to hard to deal with.

Body Dysmorphic Disorder

I'm not sure if I ever had Body Dismorphic Disorder. I was never diagnosed, but I must have been close. One year I went to visit my childhood friend. The tall, skinny blonde. The wildly popular with boys one. At that time, I didn't take into consideration that she actually looked at and talked to boys.

They had a house with a pool, and on that day my friend had a friend of hers over and we were swimming. Now, I wasn't thin, but looking back I was looking alright. I just wasn't as thin as my friend was. I heard my friend and a friend of hers whispering. "Yeah, kind of fatty around the thighs, ugh." She made a disgusted face. My friend thought it was hilarious. I was let down.

So I launched a diet regime. I was probably 15 or 16 at the time. Instead of hot food at dinner, I had salad consisting of leaf lettuce, dressing and tuna fish. Later I would cut out the tuna fish and have lettuce. I would diet drastically, cutting myself down to 600-800 calories a day. I felt fat and disgusting if I had more than 1,000 calories. Of course, this all would go fabulously for all of a few days or a week. I was starving and having a tough time keeping my mind off food. Commericals, home cooked food, stuff other people talked about… it sounded so lovely to me. I'd day dream about food. Mmmmm, chocolate cake with whipped cream. And then I'd scold myself. Didn't I want to be thin? Didn't I want to prove something to my friend, that I could be thin and pretty like she was?

Soon I'd give up and splurge. Binge eat in a serious way. I'd have my splurge and then I'd splurge more. I'd think of things that I had been fantasizing about like cake, cookies, macaroni and cheese, ice cream, pizza, french fries and burgers, spaghetti, rice and pudding. I would stuff myself. And then guilt trip later. So, it was back to it. My dry toast and lettuce salads and maybe, just maybe, a whole cup and a half of hotdish for supper.

For those of you not from the midwest, hotdish is what some people might call casserole. But don't believe for a second that meat with sauce and noodles is a casserole. A casserole is the dish you bake hotdish in. Hotdish is the food. I could write a book about this subject alone, I'm sure.

Of course, after a few days of extreme diet, I'd get good and hungry and say… bake a cake at night and eat 1/3rd of it. Buy a pint of ice cream and eat it all. You get the idea by now, I'm sure. Good old starve and splurge.

For a short time, I thought people would not accept me as a person if I didn't at least match the models in magazines with their no flab abs, toothpick thighs and slim derriere. I'd examine myself naked. Fat thighs. Fat tummy. Arm fat. Cheek fat. Butt fat. Fat elbows. Fat eyelids. Fat hair. Toe fat. Fat fingernails. Fatty fatty fat fat. I saw fat everywhere on me, but oddly enough I didn't diet to my goal weight. I would always starvation diet and then binge. I would get angry at my body for retaining this weight and punch, claw and scratch myself where I felt ugly. Thinking back, what a stupid thing to do.

I may be carrying a few pounds of fat on me, but I am fortunate enough to be healthy. Keep in mind that at this time, I was probably around a woman's size 14. Not thin, but certainly not enormous. I wanted so much to force myself to throw up. I've been close to doing it on a few occasions. Some of them recent. But I know that leads to another disorder. Builimia.

What can I say? I've tried anorexia and it just doesn't work for me. That was my cheap attempt at humor. No offense to all you anorexics out there. But deep down inside, I know that isn't the healthy way of doing things. That's cheating.

Luvox Days

By the time I was in my upper teens, we all knew something had to change. And that something was my ocd. In these days, even the most simple things were hard. I'd wash possibly hundreds of times a day. I don't think I ever counted because then we'd run into good numbers and bad numbers. Yes, I have those, too. My hands were cracked and bleeding, and if they weren't, they were so dry that flexing my hands would make the skin jut up in odd angles away from my hands. Getting dressed was hard. Feet touch floor, floor is dirty, feet touch insides of slacks or skirts, body becomes contaminated. I remember once when the tv remote fell on the floor, I became so distraught that I washed it under running water. Of course, I didn't want to ruin the remote, but it seemed the right thing to do. I would rather fry the remote than have it be dirty and make me or parents sick.

The floor that to me was so dirty that I could almost feel the germs crawling up my legs. The floor is where my little cat, Josie lives. I went through a long spanse of time where I couldn't even pet her, much less pick her up without washing. It was difficult, because she'd ask me to, in that way that cats ask for things. She'd come up and make those adorable little gerbil like meows and rub my ankles. She'd stare at me and blink. She might have been wondering what my problem was. Even though she was just a cat, I didn't want her to think I was mad at her. I'd talk to her, to which she would usually only beg to be picked up or petted more. I figured a compromise. I could pick her up if I could hold her in the bottom part of my t-shirt. That way I wouldn't actually be touching her.

Cooking, which I used to like, became tourture. How could I ever be clean enough to handle food, particualarly when some foods, when it's in some states, is dirty to begin with? (Such as raw eggs and raw meat.) Being out and about, which was difficult but usually enjoyable, became tough, as defending myself against various colds became my priority instead of whatever I was doing. Eating out, even eating in general became difficult. Out, I could never be sure the dishes or glasses were clean enough. And I would pick at my food and look for imagined spots or contaminants.

I gave up on washing my face, it was just too difficult. Wiping my face after eating, too,was hard. The germs that I couldn't seem to get off of my hands might jump onto my face and might make me sick. Showering became difficult, and sometimes more than once a day.

At this point you might be asking yourself why I did these things. The answer is simply becase the touture of doing these rituals was better than the tourture of the anxiety that would be present if I didn't. I hated my ocd and loved it at the same time.

When my parents would insist on helping me out of my ocd, the fear of the anxiety would kick in. I wasn't ready to work on my issues yet. I would say things like how the ocd was my friend. Keeping me safe, and at the same time, it kept me dreading simple things like eating, bathing and washing my face, and took enjoyment away from my hobbies.

As much as I wanted friends, I didn't reach out to people. I had the fear, and still do, that what I say might have offended someone. Or might have sounded stupid. So I was quiet a lot. Plus, I wasn't really focusing at all. I was too preoccupied with keeping myself safe. I would clean things. Sometimes soap and water with a rinse and dry stage. Sometimes with bleach. I remember bleaching the plastic desk phone and wondering why it felt warm after I did.

Doing my housework was a chore, but in more ways than it would be to your average teen. A certain numbers of passes with the vaccum cleaner. Keeping "bad" thoughts out of your mind while doing housework, or having to redo it. Washing and drying clothes was difficult and required multiple hand washings. Pretty soon, all I had to do as far as the laundry was concerned was fold and put away my clothes, and that became difficult, too. Hands had to be clean enough. Drawer handles and pulls had to be clean. Insides of drawers had to be clean. I started counting in my head, trying to land on certain combinations of numbers. One, shake the wrinkles out, two find the shoulders, three fold in half, four fold in half the other way... and on and on it went.

Even walking had a ritual. Not stepping on cracks outside. Hitting the edge of the rugs in the house in the right part of my foot at the right numbers when walking. I would be so exhausted at the end of the day.

I used to enjoy staying up and watching tv or being online, but with all that do deal with, I wanted to go to bed early and sleep in. Being awake meant having to fight with some urge or another. It was then we knew I needed something.

It was a long fight with me to get me to try it. Of course, wanting to be well informed, I read up on the drug. It was used to treat ocd, but it also had side affects. A lot of them. I read the tiny print and it scared me. I remember having my prescription filled. I was nervous and my dad took the first pill to show me it was alright. I felt oddly important, too. It was my first prescription, these little yellow football shaped pills. It came on a slip of paper with fancy writing on it from the doctor. I felt grown up turning it in. The first few pills I took I was instantly more cheery. Help was on the way.

On Luvox

On Luvox, I didn't worry as much. At first it was so wonderful. But there was a downside. I was only on half of the recommended dose and yet, instead of worrying, I seemed to have no energy. I used to pursue things, hobbies, when I had time for them in between my bouts of worrying, but on Luvox all I seemed to care about was getting done with whatever absolutely needed to be done for the time.

In my off times, I remember one thing I liked to do was to slump over the back edge of my couch. I had a couch with its back towards a window. I would slump over the back of it, legs sprawled out behind me and look outside. It was comfortable and seemed like a good thing to do.

I was 17 or 18 at the time and just learning to drive. Sometimes I would be so tired from the drug that I would unwisely drive with one eye open. Not that I wanted to, just that my eyelids were that heavy. I'd crack the window open to get some air moving around so I wouldn't fall asleep.

I'd fall asleep easily during the day. This is something that normally doesn't happen easily for me.

Other things were changing too. I used to be extra frugal. I was Ms. Cheapskate. I paid off my first car loan six months early. But on the Luvox, I was a different person. I saw stuff, at first small impulse buys at the store. Then larger things. Things I knew I didn't have a balance in my checkbook for. But it didn't matter to me. I didn't care. I wanted whatever it was. I'd buy it. These were the days when you could still "float" check for a day or two. I'd scrape up some money, sometimes even the spare change in my bank, and deposit it. Sometimes I just flat out didn't want to do it. So I'd wait and get overdrafts. So what. I had a credit card. So what? I'd spend money that was supposed to go for necessities. So what? I had a credit card. It didn't matter to me any more. My spending became out of control.

Driving, which I had struggled with anyway, having near panic attacks while driving in traffic, became even more tricky. I would go on red lights. I just wasn't in a condition to be paying attention. I didn't care. I was so tired I could barely keep my eyes open. I wanted to get home as soon as possible to unload my impulse buys and nap.

Also something else I noticed was even though I didn't worry like I used to... I didn't feel happy either. I was an emotional zombie. I wanted off of the Luvox in a bad way, but at the same time I knew that by getting off of it, the worries and rituals would return. I hadn't stopped the rituals all the way while I was on the Luvox anyway. But at least they were more bearable than they had been.

At the time, I told myself I needed to come up with a coping strategy. I told myself that I would ask myself when I started to worry if this thought would have bothered me while I was on Luvox. If the answer was no, I would tell myself that "if it looks like a duck and quacks like a duck, it must be ocd, let it go..." That mantra worked for a long time.

But I ran into another issue. My prescribing doctor wouldn't tell me how to back down off of the Luvox. Instead they sent me a padded envelope with 7 or 8 little bottles of another drug. I had asked to get off of the one I was on, and here I was sitting around with another drug they wanted me to take at the same time. No, thank you. My parents and myself remember how I got on the Luvox to begin with. I had been taking two pills. I backed down to one and a half. After a few weeks, down to one. A few weeks after that, half. And then off altogether.

Now I expect that the medication works fine on some people. It just wasn't my answer. As it turns out, I'm sensitive to selective serotonin reuptake inhibitors like Luvox.

That "Just Right" Feeling

Of the things that I'm most upset at myself for, this next item would be high on the list. I used to think things had to be "just right" before I could fully enjoy them. It usually revolved around how I felt about my appearance. Should I go to town, or shouldn't I? No, town is a treat for the thin and fashionable and I felt fat and clumsy. A special event would arrive and I would pick on myself for wearing the wrong clothes. Or I hadn't worn makeup. Or I didn't like my hair. The list went on and on, and even during the fun I would think to myself, "Oh, this is fun. But now I hope we re-do this soon so that I can have everything "just right" so that I can really enjoy things."

I would marvel at people who seemed to just enjoy things as they were. I made the assumption that they must naturally be happy with how things were. That they had achieved their "just right" and had things together.

I often wonder if ocd ties into perfectionism somehow. Perfectionism can be a double edged sword. Perfectionism helps you to deliever quality work and focus on goals. However, perfectionism can turn on you and make it so things don't seem to be "good enough". Therefore, things can become burdensome and drudgery. Even things once enjoyed can turn into a torment when they aren't "good enough". Perfectionism can turn from your friend into an enemy by turning you into a procrastinator who is ever in search of feeling "just right".

The Social Column

When I was 19, I made friends with a girl in the area. I didn't know her too well and we only hung out a few times. I half kidded... did she know any cute, single guys. She smiled and said maybe. Awhile later, she hooked me up with a pal of hers. Let's call him Kung-fuey.

Now, this was my first date, my first "real" boyfriend. Of course, I'd chatted with boys online before, but I hadn't had a face to face date. I could sit here and tell you it was because of the cliquey area. That might be true, but also I was not at all confident. I'm curvey and have a tummy. I have dark hair. I have glasses. I was of the idea that men wanted women that looked like my childhood friend. Tall, thin and blonde. Not me.

At the time, I didn't chalk anything up to attitude. So, I plain old didn't approach guys unless I had to. You know, things like where's the bathroom, or how much is that. Other ligitmate questions.

I chatted with Kung-fuey online a few times, and then met him in person. I stopped by the grocery store where he worked. He scooped me up in a bear hug that felt more like fighting with an octopus. We agreed that our next date would be at my place. I didn't drive at the time, so it seemed logical. I would learn later that inviting guys to "your place" is almost the same as saying "would you have sex with me", unless you worded it right. So Kung-fuey came over... we took a walk where my first kiss was having my nose bitten. I stared at him. He acted like I was stupid. We walked and he talked. Most of what he said sounded like it came out of a video game. We sat and talked. He told how good he was in bed. How his ex-girlfriend wanted sex all the time because he was that hot. How she wanted this, how she wanted that from him, how she broke his bed. On and on and on. I couldn't think of a polite way to ask him to leave already. He hugged me. Oddly enough I didn't mind that. The hugging felt nice. He kissed me, my first kiss that was a kiss. It felt nice and besides it's something I wanted to do anyway. He got more and more pressuring to me. I said no, which he respected. He then proceeded to expose himself in front of me. I was shocked. But what could I say? *Put that away? I'll have to clean for hours if you do that.* I was stunned. I guess I hadn't thought of what to do in a situation like this. I was quiet. It was better than him making me do stuff with him anyway. I didn't know what exactly to do, so I moved to a chair and watched. He got done. My mind immediately flew to... what if there is something left over from him on my floor? What if I step in it, and getting dressed I get some on my underwear and get pregnant. He finally left. He said he hoped he hadn't messed me up worse than before I met him. I don't know what my reply was, or if I said anything.

I had a lot of mixed feelings about that encounter. I felt disloyal to myself for letting things get a little out of hand with someone that I knew I didn't really even like. Later, I would realize that this kind of thing happens. It's practically a right of passage for some.

I showered for a long time after he left and hopped across my floor on one foot to get dressed. I broke it off after that with Kung-fuey, but this experience launched my most embarassing fear. The pregnancy fear.

First Comes Love, Then Comes Marriage, Then Comes...

… the pregnancy fear.

After my little situation with Kung-fuey, I began imagining all the ways I could get pregnant without having sex. What about the beaches that I used to love going swimming at? It was lake water, so no chemicals. What if there was something, sperm from some random guy, and it would float to me. I would get pregnant. Of course, in my mind I knew that this was highly unlikely, maybe even impossible, but my overactive imagination took over. I imagined getting morning sickness, and then gaining a baby belly as the baby grew. People would know I was pregnant. I would feel sick, and gain weight for nine months, and then I would finally have the baby, the painful birth process. What would I do with the child? Would I give him/her out to be adopted? Would I keep him/her?

Other than Kung-fuey, I hadn't really dated. I wasn't that popular with men, which I now realize was mainly due to my attitude. I ignored them and treated most attention from them as though it was coming from a negative standpoint. I'd see someone looking at me and think *"Fine! I don't like you either."*

But somewhere in me, I knew that I wanted a relationship. And here I would have a child.

I didn't drive for a long time, and living in the middle of the country, that means that you have to be dependent on others to go where you want. You have to carefully plan for things you want to do. Now with a baby that would get much more difficult. I imagined that people would look down on me. I would probably gain a lot of weight, something I have an issue with anyway, and now, after the baby I would be even heavier and less attractive than before. And who knows what the baby would be like. It would be half its mystery dad. Maybe he was a jerk. All because one day I went swimming at the beach. But who, other than my parents who knew I didn't date, would know that? Girl gets pregnant from swimming? Unheard of! People would probably assume I was a slut. Me. Someone who avoided men like they were strange, alien creatures. Me, who under normal conditions, only spoke to them when the conditions absolutely called for it. I almost couldn't stand it.

Of course, what made the pregnancy fear so much worse was the fact that I hadn't been getting periods regularly. Other women seemed to know when theirs would come within a day or two. On the other hand, I had no clue. I might get mine two months in a row. And then skip the next six. This was one physical symptom I didn't bother to read about for a long time. Usually my ocd had me study up on whatever symptoms I had (cough, bruises, etc…), but this one I didn't. In my mind there was only probably one thing that could cause a woman to miss her periods like that. Pregnancy. Things besides the lake and the floor (even though it had been months since Kung-fuey was over) got me nervous. What about those shared bathrooms? You know, the ones with one stall, where either a man or woman could use them. What if there was random sperm on the toilet paper? What if there was random sperm on objects? Or on public chairs?

I became paranoid, but the symptoms of my paranoia were similar to the common cold and rabies fear which I still had at the same time. Washing. Showering. Getting dressed became difficult, more so. I would hop on one foot, from the bathroom to my bedroom after showering, then I would open my underwear drawer and wash my hands. Hop back, pick out a pair of panties, stuff the upper edge into my mouth and hop over to my sock bin. Put on a pair of socks, wash my hands and then, finally, put the underwear on. Pants were just about as trying.

Later, I would learn that my missed periods were because of a hormonal imbalance, and that women with this condition usually have to struggle to get pregnant with fertility drugs, timing and sometimes even invitro fertilization. Thinking back, I'm so happy I got over the pregnancy fear. Ironic isn't it, that my missed periods weren't from some mystery pregnancy. They were from something that will be likely to actually make it difficult for me to get pregnant, if and when I want to start a family of my own.

Internet Love

I was not quite technical enough to be a geek, but I did come close. Other eighteen and nineteen year olds probably stayed out and partied. I stayed up until the wee hours teaching myself HTML, the language that webpages are written in. I made my own websites. Tons of them. About me. About horses. About bands and TV shows that I liked. I updated them weekly and then monthly. What a thrill.

I had been contacted by some strange men. Sometimes it felt good to be wanted even if it came from men who might be among some of the strangest to walk the earth. At least I was getting attention. I didn't wish to meet them, I just liked the attention. One guy pushed it too far when he told me he was having fantasies about this fourteen year old girl and that, if I wanted to, we could type out these fantasies to each other, with me pretending I was fourteen. That was disgusting. I include it to give an example of some of the truly strange people who roam the world wide web.

I wasn't worried about these men finding me. In the middle of the country it would be hard to find me. Even people that we wanted to have as guests had a difficult time finding the place.

I should have figured that it would be only time until I found someone I did want to meet. I was on a music message board, and there he was. Let's call him Bisq. Bisq was from England and played guitar, and liked the same music as I did.

A few times, my ocd had gotten so severe that I had to go stay at a crisis center. At the time, I think my parents and I thought it was going to be like some kind of extended in-patient ocd therapy for me. But as we found out, the crisis center is sort of like a holding tank. People with problems they can't handle on their own go there. A doctor talks to you for admitting purposes, and if you're lucky, they might even follow up. Otherwise, the rest of the time you're pretty much left on your own.

You have a bedroom, and a shared living room and kitchenette and shared bathroom. That shared bathroom especially got to me.

Other than meals and showering, you were pretty much left to your own devices.

Some of the staff were wonderful. There was one young woman who I really hope pursued psychiatric nursing. Then there were some not so wonderful staff who were likely there only for their pay check. Sometimes they tried. During the day they'd see who wanted to go for a walk. Sometimes they would bring me some informational videos to watch about ocd.

But for the entirety of the day, you were pretty well alone. You could watch tv if they visiting area/living room wasn't full. You could stare out your window. You could sit at your desk. I wrote a lot of journal entries at that desk. It seemed like the most interesting thing to do.

It was after my return home from one of these experiences that I started chatting with Bisq. He noticed my abscense from the message boards and sent me a private message. He missed me. I told him what had happened. I told him that I had a problem with anxiety. And he answered me. My anxiety issue didn't seem to bother him, not one little bit. He'd seen pictures of me too, so my looks probably didn't bother him either. It was an amazing thought to me. We wrote back and forth. He was intelligent and witty. Good looking and well spoken. We'd type letters… hi, how are you? And we'd mix in our own fictional stories. Rated G or PG, of course. Bisq was a gentleman. Or so I thought.

He broke up with his girlfriend, and then he told me everything I wanted to hear. He thought I was beautiful. He thought I was smart. All of a sudden other guys looking at me didn't bother me. Who cared what they thought when Bisq thought I was pretty and smart. I started staying home to chat with him, and, when we weren't chatting or writing to each other, I was thinking about him.

Then he went and did something that really made me fall for him. He told me that he had made it his New Year's resolution to come and visit me. I was elated. I felt like dancing through my days. Of course, this wasn't going to happen right away. He needed to get some money together to come here. He never asked me point blank for money, but there were hints.

Of course, my ocd wouldn't let it rest either. I started worrying for him. Any little delay in him getting back to me meant I would worry. Was my dear friend Bisq alright? Had something dreadful happened to him? Where was he anyway? Was he starting to be disinterested? Keep in mind I never meant to be clingy or annoying. But I was worried. My overactive ocd imagination kicked into gear. My dear handsome Bisq laying alone in some hospital with a case of amnesia. My online boyfriend being mugged and then left unconscious in an alleyway. No one would contact me about him if any of this did happen. How could they?

The only form of communication we shared was online chatting and e-mails. I'd pray he was alright, and then I'd have to get the prayers just right in order to feel confidant that God would answer them and keep my boyfriend safe. One time I remember praying all throughout a meal. We had prayed out loud together as a family, then I had said a silent prayer. I didn't word it just right so I prayed again. And again. And again. And again. Since I wasn't eating, my parents started to notice something was up. I opened my eyes and took a bite. And then prayed again as I stared into space. They tried talking to me. I still wasn't getting my prayer right and, with each repetition, I would get more anxious. I didn't want my parents to help me, because to me just about any help offered for my ocd felt like scolding. I answered them with the briefest possible answers, in between prayers. I took bites of food in between prayers. I got it right by the end of that meal. I also took to chanting. A bad thought would flash in my head. A battered and bleeding Bisq lying in a street somewhere, and in my mind I would think these words. ...healthy well... alive well... healthy well. In that order, over and over again. I felt I had to mutter them out loud, even if out loud meant the quietest of whispers. I finally got that down to an art where I could whisper it without moving my lips. Just by moving my tongue on the roof of my mouth, I could make the faintest sounds of my chant ... healthy well... alive well... healthy well... I had to continue my chant for him whenever the mood would strike. During meals, during shopping, when I was online, when I was outside, when I was talking to other people, and even when my childhood friend came to visit me.

Between praying and chanting, it got intense. I would worry and sometimes cry out of my fear for what had happened to my friend. If I didn't hear from him one day, I was down and lethargic. I'd get an e-mail from him the next day and be elated. And so the cycle would go. I didn't want to turn into Ms. Clingy, but the worry was driving me up the wall. I tried gently explaining to him that when I didn't hear from him it made my ocd flair up. I asked him for permission to stop worrying. He didn't give it to me. He repeated that old phrase about the best psychiatric doctors only being able to help you find the answer within yourself. So my praying for him and chanting continued.

All of a sudden I noticed strange things. I'd sign on to the instant messenger we used to chat, and he'd be online! I was instantly happy. As I'd go to say hi to him, he'd appear offline. It happened a few times and I chalked it up to timing. Who knows, with the time difference and all, he was probably going to run some errands. Or go to bed. Or whatever. The more it happened, I grew suspicious.

Finally our relationship ended. He told me he had found this beautiful girl (who yes, had some opposite physical features from me) and that her family was wealthy and she had traveled there to England to meet him. I was astounded. He compared her looks to a certain popular actress and, even though this was years ago, I still cringe when I hear her name or see her on tv.

I was raised to tell people the truth. When you said something big, like how you wanted to meet someone, and that you had feelings for them, you meant it. You didn't mean to just toy with them. I was devistated. I had spent all that time on him. Not just writing to and about him, but thought time. During the time our online relationship was going strong, I thought about him almost all day and all night. Things I did, all of a sudden, were about him. "I know, if I go to the bagel shop, I can tell Bisq about it! We might even go here together when he comes over..."

Yes, perhaps I was obsessed, and perhaps I had grown clingy with all of my worry. I was naïve. I thought all people meant what they said. I was just stunned when I found out that they didn't. I grew even less confident around men. It took me a long time to to get over it.

Of course, through the years there have been other online and real life boyfriends. But I'll never forget the lesson Bisq taught me. People don't always mean what they say.

Light Me Up

One night my parents and I were watching a classic movie about someone who had been poisoned by some luminous toxin. By the time he knew something was wrong, the poison had too much of a foothold on him and there was nothing anyone could do for him. This gave my ocd mind the foothold it needed to really get to work.

The blurb at the end of the movie said that this glowing toxin was real. I began to imagine I saw glowing bits in my food. Hard candy became hard to eat. I needed to shield it in my hands first to make sure it didn't glow. And then if it were in a shiny wrapper, that would catch my eye.

As with the previous examples, I really did know that any chance of that particular toxin having contaminated that particular candy was highly unlikely. But still the what if was at work, and driving me crazy. I'd start seeing glowing bits in drinks, particularly dark soda, like cola. That drove me insane.

Pretty soon other non-food items became subject to my obsessive compulsive disorder. New toothbrushes might have been sprayed in the glowing poison. I would turn out all the lights and take the desired item out in the dark. Of course, if there were any little amount of light in the room I would start worrying. The light is coming from under the door, not from the object, I would tell myself. And it made sense. It was logical.

But, of course, there was the big "what if" left to deal with. In this case, the what if was what if the light was actually coming from the imagined luminous toxins on my toothbrush, hard candy, or other food item.

Pretty soon food with odd colors that I used to like, such as pickles and blue slushies, became off limits. It might be a good idea to limit such unnatural colors in your diet. But not for the reasons I did. I thought they were glowing and didn't want to take the chance that they might have been luminous, even though I could see with my own eyes that my food, toothbrush and lipsticks weren't glowing.

Trust and the Radio

I think a lot of ocd may be the innability to trust yourself. Checking things the way I used to check my cd player may be evidence of this. Though I don't consider checking to be on of my "main" ocd symptoms, I did have a bout of checking the cd player.

As a music crazy teen, and adult for that matter, of course I enjoyed playing the cds that I was crazy for. And it would all be fine until it was time to go somewhere. Was the cd player off? I mean really off? Really, really? Of course, I could hear it wasn't playing, but the power could still be on. Or I could have simply turned the volume down. Or, I could've pushed pause. The possibilites racked up. I'd stare at the window of cd player. It was off. I could see it was off. I'd stare and tell myself, "It's off". But it wasn't good enough. I'd run my finger over the switch for radio, cassette or cd. It was in the radio position, not the more scary cd or cassette positions.

To my overtasked mind, I thought it would be easier to start a fire with a cd player switched to cassette or cd than to radio. After all people sometimes leave home with a radio playing. A paused cd or cassette tape, however, maybe could create stress within the unit itself. At least that was my reasoning. I ran my finger around the power button. "It's off", I yelled at myself in my head. But the doubt wouldn't leave. And of course, touching the power button made me wonder if I had accidently turned it on. And on it would go.

"We're ready to go", my parents would yell, and I would panic. "Just a minute", I'd reply as I strided in a fast and determined pace towards my door. All the ocd had to say is "what if". I would stand in the doorway looking at the cd player. "It's off", I'd tell myself again, only in a weaker tone of voice... "It's off", I would plead with my ocd.

I know I said above that not being able to trust yourself is part of ocd, but as I think more, the second part of it must be overactive imagination.

In this fear, as with so many of the other ones, my mind was busy exploring what could happen. And I'd picture all sorts of things in minute details. We'd be driving and the cd player would start to smoke. I imagined the disc spinning around inside as the lazer used to read the disc would be burning a hole through it. Smoke would be pouring out of my giant stereo by now. And then... sparks! And then a small fire would start. My cat would run to the other end of the house as the fire engulfed my office and bedroom. Eventually the fire would spread. My cat would probably just pass out from the smoke. The fish in the aquarium would be boiled. Precious and irreplaceable things like photos would be burned. We'd come home and the house would be burnt down.

The fire marshall would investigate and, in a serious tone of voice, tell my parents that it had come from the cd player ... and then... in slow motion... the fire marshall would turn and point to me... *the fire came the cd player in her room!*

I'd apologize over and over again. My parents would be, of course, enraged at me. I feared I would be disowned, and I feared that what my low self esteem had been telling me: that I was stupid and that I was useless, would be true after all. Who knows where I would go or what I would do. Extended relatives for the most part didn't get along with us or lived far away. I would probably go to a homeless shelter. My future would probably be a bag lady. I'd have to sort through garbage to eat, and sleep in rubble. And I wouldn't have enough money for soap or access to a shower. Some grubby homeless man might rape me and then I'd be pregnant, dirty and smelly.

When I think back on it, the fire fear really did ignite a lot of other fears, too. Fear of germs, fear of pregnancy are in there too. All that mental strife because of a cd player.

Sci-fi

At times I wondered if most science fiction writers didn't have ocd. My overactive mind certainly kept me imagining stories. Sometimes elaborate theories. For example:

I was wearing my blue sweater at the grocery store and someone coughed.

I put my clothes away, I forgot to throw them in the hamper.

My blue sweater touched my orange t-shirt on one side and my white shirt on the other side.

Now, not only is my blue sweater dirty from mystery cough contamination, so is my orange t-shirt and my white shirt.

Take them all to the hamper. They must all be washed.

Now, scrub hands vigorously.

Now I have to change shirts, because carrying the armful of contaminated shirts contaminted the one I was wearing.

Take off the contaminated shirt.

Contaminated shirt rubs against my face and hair as I pull it off over my head.

Soap, wash and scrub hands, arms, face and hair.

Pick another shirt to wear.

Since blue sweater caused so much worry, worry about wearing blue.

Look aimlessly over closet for some non-anxiety provoking item of clothing.

Panic because all clothing somehow doesn't "feel" right.

Decide on a shirt. Wear for approximately 3 minutes, and then have a bad thought. Change shirt and think a good thought to undo the bad thought.

Throw 3 minute shirt into hamper.

Almost on the brink of tears, stare into closet and try to choose a non-anxiety provoking shirt.

Of course, there are almost countless stories like this. But then there are some *really* strange things.

My parents and I watched a movie where aliens overtake human bodies in an effort to overtake the world. They would infect people, and then as the people slept, the aliens would slowly overtake their bodies. The only thing that could defeat the aliens was water.

After watching it, I would feel mystery sensations on my skin. Like little droplets of water.

At this point I would like to interject that, in my experience, ocd can be wonderfully sensual. I have felt things so many times. Sprays of water hitting my face. Stuff crawling up my leg.

The sensation of being physically dirty or sticky even though I wasn't. I wonder if the sensations are real, or are they my hyperactively primed ocd.

Anyways, this time I wondered if it was happening. The aliens coming to inhabate me. For some reason, just rinsing in water wasn't challenging enough for me. When I would get these sensations or thoughts, I thought the "cure" for not getting inhabited by aliens overnight was to make my eyes water. Usually staring point blank into a lightbulb accomplished this. I do remember standing, balancing on the edge of my bed, staring into a ceiling light fixture. My eyes would water and I'd feel relieved. Ah. No alien invasion tonight.

Another ocd ritual that was worthy of it's own sci-fi book or movie was the soul stealing camera. Once, on a family trip to Duluth, I saw another family taking pictures at some of the landmarks. I panicked. I thought that somehow their camera had the power to steal not only my soul, but my very body.

It would wait until I was asleep, that way I wouldn't be conscious. I wouldn't be awake to fight the currents of the soul stealing camera. I would be sucked into their camera, in a still photo. The lady in the background. They would have the photo printed, and from the negative I would call out to the film processing people. "Help me! I'm stuck in here!", my newly small voice would say, and my reverse colored image would jump around. Of course, no one would notice. I'd get printed and be stuck in a photo. I'd be put in a frame or album somewhere. I'd pace around the photo, taken in a park. I'd go up to the people in the photo and try talking to them, but they would be like mannequins, of course. They were only images of people. And, when people would look into the photo, I'd wave my hands and yell and jump, but no one would notice or help. After all, I was just the lady in the background who couldn't seem to move into the foreground and get helped back to the real world. In a way, it might have been my own mind feeling trapped by the ocd.

Though the contamination theories remained, the alien fear and the camera fear left me rather quickly. I realized at the time that they were utterly ridiculous. I felt stupid doing the rituals, and I felt stupid for even thinking these things up. But it still didn't help. The fear still felt real, and even though I was tormented by these ridiculous thoughts, I couldn't help but laugh. "This is really precious, Frederique. You're standing on your bed trying to get your eyes to water to prevent aliens from living in your body. What next?"

Impressions

Ocd has the impressive ability to make others form opinions about you. When a person is anxious, they tend to "pull out" of the moment and dwell in the future or maybe the past. People notice this kind of glossy exsistence. And there is always the chance of getting caught doing an ocd ritual. But there are other ways ocd can humiliate the people who have it. I'll use this example from a recent summer trip.

Yearly my parents and aunt and uncle enjoy a small town's city celebration in Northern Minnesota. On the weekend of this event, the small little town becomes a bustle of activity. There are a few picnic tables in a shelter and you have to be quick if you want one around lunch time. This year we were fortunate enough to grab a table. Or should I say, a part of a table. People tend to cram onto these picnic tables so tightly that you're rubbing elbows and possibly thighs with complete strangers. Well, along comes this *really, really quite large* lady. I'm a full figured woman myself, but this lady was like approximately three of me. I didn't care about her size, but I knew that with her size, it would be a tight squeeze for her to sit at one of the only oepn spots at the table. Next to me. I didn't mind the fact that she was large, but what I did mind were the sores on her forearm. I freaked out. My face must have reflected it because the guy sitting across from me just kind of smirked and nodded at me. He must have thought that I was "freaking out" because she was big. I hoped she didn't see it. I got up and jogged to the nearest restroom to wash. I still hope I didn't hurt that woman's feelings.

Men

And I really used to misjudge men. I think I owe roughly half of the world's population an apology. I am not sure if my odd attitude was due to ocd or to an early girlhood experience. No, I wasn't raped or sexually abused in any way. But some old family friends used to believe in a polygamous lifestyle.

This was a married couple, and there was only one wife. But they were open to more. Now it wasn't that issue that confused me. I personally would not judge someone who lives that lifestyle, as long as noone is forced into it, and as long as there were no bulk marriages of fourteen year old girls or something like that. I was eleven at the time. I remember being cautioned to be careful and keep my distance when I was around the man in the relationship. I wondered why, because he would joke with me, and nothing seemed strange. And then I found out that he had asked, casually, if he could marry me. It reminded me as though he were checking out a book at a library.

Of course, my dad did not agree. He could see past that man's motives. I do not think the man wanted an ultra young bride. I think the man desired a farm similar to where I grew up. I think this because he would later say things like that.

I developed a strange fear of men. I was attracted to them, but I felt that I could be sold or given away at a moments notice. Of course, I knew my dad wouldn't do that to me. But I felt that if I dated a guy, even just once, then that was it. I couldn't date anyone else. I was his, almost as sure as I was married.

I would imagine myself in a loveless marriage with a guy who had many families. Occasionally pregnant and providing him with more children, keeping his house and bringing in money for him. So I avoided men.

Of course, my other fear was fear of rape. I must admit, I've never been assulted or raped, but I had this odd fear of it. In my mind 99.99999998% of men only wanted sex from women. Even talking to them, or looking at them, could lead to a man dragging me off in the woods and brutally raping me.

My imagination, and I call it imagination because I have no clue if indeed this was some paranoid imagination of mine or truly ocd, was of the pure obsession variety. People with pure obsessions ruminate, but do not have a ritual to perform to relieve their anxiety. I didn't have a ritual as to my fear of men, other than avoiding them.

The pregnancy fear was in the background, too. I don't believe in abortion, so I would be big, fat and pregnant with a rapist's child. The rest of my life raising someone because of an attack on me. I imagined it.

When I was sixteen I knew I wanted to play guitar. I took lessons. It was a scary possibility. Being alone, in a small little room with one of *them*. A man. Might I add that this little room, a music studio, was *soundproofed*. The first few lessons were tense. I remember not wanting to look him in the eye. I remember him telling me to look at him. After awhile, I got to know him. And you know, he wasn't scary. He wasn't going to force me to marry him, and he wasn't going to rape me.

My other bias against men was completely opposite. As I grew a little older, I figured out that's not how the world works. Men don't expect a vow of faithfulness on the first date. In fact, some men are rather picky about who they date.

I went from, in effect putting myself on a pedestal by assuming that men wanted to marry me against my wishes or to rape me, to knocking myself down. Whenever guys would look at me, I would assume that they were thinking something negative, like, "Look at her! She's ugly, and fat. Probably stupid, too. Oh look, she's looking at me. She probably is attracted to me. In her dreams!" Then they would look at their friends and smile or laugh. Who knows, in reality it probably wasn't even about me, but to me this seemed to confirm the fact, that yes, they were laughing at me.

I would avoid looking at guys, and if I would happen to, I would already be on the defensive. I would think, "Fine, I don't like you either", and scowl. On the rare occasion that I would actually make eye contact with guys, the negative times stood out in my mind. Like the time I saw a guy at a restaurant.

On my way to the restroom I smiled at him. He smiled back. On the way walking back to my table, he was talking to some preppie looking girl. Laughing. He made a gesture at his teeth and they looked over at me. This was before I had braces, so I had a bit of an overbite. I remember feeling so angry at him, and then low self esteem at myself. I don't like to admit that some stupid encounter like that shaped my future experiences and self confidence with men, but maybe it did.

Of course, some nice things happened too. At the same restaurant a different guy whom I didn't know walked up to me, and gave me a cross necklace he'd made out of beads. He said, "Merry Christmas", in the middle of summer and walked out. Those things don't seem to stick as much as the negative.

I finally figured out that men, other than anatomical differences, aren't that much different than women in the effect that there are some bad. There are some scary. And there are some that are truly nice. They are human beings, like me. Not scary aliens. I realize that now, but still struggle with the self esteem issue. I feel unattractive. Now I'm the first to say that I'm no model, but when I look the mirror I feel a sense of relief, because my eyes tell me that I don't look as homely as I think I do.

Playing By the Numbers

To add more demented fun to my torment, I developed a fear of certain "bad" numbers. "Bad numbers" are related to something bad that has happened to me, in some way. I don't even want to write what mine are, but I'll give you some of my "bad numbers" in a form that I feel safe typing them, as math problems.

9+1

8+3

9+3

9+4

20+4+1

51 + 1+1+1

91+1

34+2

It's surprising where numbers can appear when you're not looking for them. Oh, sure there's the usual digital clock displays, those huge digital thermometers that banks put up, check book balances, bills, invoices, TV and radio channels, price tags and menu prices. All the regular places you'd look for numbers. But there are also somewhat less obvious places for numbers. License plates, food packages and clothing sizes.

Then there are numbers that aren't visual numbers. There are mental numbers. I used to count as I would walk. It wouldn't happen on purpose. It would just happen. 1,2,3,4,5,6,7,8,9,... I would pause. Getting close to a bad number. I would just start over at one. I didn't want to count. *Please just stop counting. Alright, we'll stop counting. Here goes,... not counting... 5,6,7,8... alright, I'll just stop from there. Wait... I started at five, I should re-start at one...*

And there is the number of times as compared to the number of previous times. I usually make three swipes with the vacuum cleaner in front of the stairs. So, in other words, the next time I vacuum, I can't make 4+2 swipes, because 34+2 is a bad number. So it would be three one time, and six the next. Put the three in front of 4+2, and it's a bad number. See? I still currently do that one.

Oddly enough, the only place I still seem to count vacuuming swipes is in front of the stairs. I used to do doorways, too.

And there are so many others. Numbers of pumps of soap. Numbers of steps. Numbers of numbers. So now I try to avoid looking at digital clocks. Not always easy. If I happen to look at a clock while doing something, anything... housework, writing, whatever else... and see a bad nmber, I have to fight the urge to either:

1.)   Re-do whatever I was doing when the clock changes to a good number,

or

2.)   Refuse to do whatever I was doing for the rest of the day.

Sometimes I wind up rather limited in what I can do during the day.

One of the most unusal ways the number fear manifested itself in me was in toilet paper usage. That's right. I counted sheets. Couldn't have a bad number. One night I spent a considerable amount of time flushing sheets of toilet paper down. Happily I think I stopped counting toilet paper sheets after that. It was just too hard and too wasteful.

And, of course, there's always the total of your bill whether shopping or eating out. Normally I avoid items that are priced "bad" numbers. But the total is much harder to figure out, how much tax there would be, and me not being brilliant at math by any means. The easy answer is to add on a pack of mints or some other small impulse buy. I've been able to overcome this several times.

But the numbers truly are exhasuting. Then after the ocd gets bored of plain old numbers, you can always move into sets of numbers. They can tie themselves to other ocd rituals making everything at least two times as difficult. This is no longer as problematic for me, but I still have my flair ups.

In fact, recently I was booking a hotel room at a local casino. I'd never been there, but I had signed up for the player's discount club online. The total for the room should have come to around $51.00. But, in an especially cheery voice, the woman informed me that with my player's club discount I would owe $46.66. I nearly fell of my chair. I, and many others with the fear of certain numbers, find the number six-hundred and sixty-six particularly scary because the Bible mentions that it's the number of the Beast. I so badly wanted to pay full price instead. "Uh," I stammered…, "I've not been to your casino before, so

I don't think I'm a player's club member." The helpful voice on the other end of the line informed me that I had indeed signed up online, and she gave me the date. There was no way I could argue with that, and even if I did argue with that, I would likely be lying. And having scrupulosity, I try to safeguard against doing that. But that's another chapter.

The woman on the phone proceeded to walk me through how to go about picking up my player's club card. I couldn't help but notice that she sounded happy to give me the discount that I didn't want. I realized that she had no way of knowing that certain numbers might bother certain people. So what happened? I took the discount. Why? Because I realized right then and there that the only way numbers have any meaning or any "power" is because people give them power. And I'm not letting ocd rule me. Not this time.

You Can't Have My Hobbies

My ocd has pushed me out of a lot of my hobbies. Photography used to get to me. You can't wash a camera. I so enjoyed going to parks and taking photos outdoors.

One time I put the camera down right next to some bird droppings. Panic siezed me, even though I hadn't actually put the camera in the bird doo. There was no easy way to wash my hands at a park, and in those days I didn't trust hand sanitizer. Besides, this meant that the camera was now "dirty". What was I to do? I felt instantly exhausted. I wanted to cry. And then I talked back to the ocd. *"You can't have my hobbies. You've taken away so much of my time and energy, you cannot take my hobbies, too."* I felt like a weight was lifted off my shoulders. It didn't take all of the fear away, but it helped. It wasn't always easy. I still have to fight to keep my hobbies in the present day.

Another example is music. Remember my "numbers"? I read tableture, the notes are represented as numbers. Sometimes when my number fear flairs, I find it excruciating to practice, even though I want to. I even quit guitar lessons with my special guitar teacher. Numbers in gutiar tab, turned into number of songs played, number of times I played a song, and number of words in the title. It was tormenting and tiresome and turned something I used to enjoy into something dreadful.

More currently, I've been able to overcome the numbers. It's now the scrupulosity that kicks in. Scrupulosity is a fear having to do with spirituality, religion and/or ethics.

Before I practice anything else, I feel I need to play a Christian song. That would be fine in and of itself. But the ocd kicks in. During the song I might have a bad thought. *"I don't want to do this"*, I think to myself. I panic instantly. Of course, I want to play this Christian song. I stop and pray lengthy repetitive prayers. "GOD please forgive me. I do want to play this song. I do want to praise you. Christian music is crap! No! No! GOD forgive me. I didn't mean that! Christian music is... is... well it isn't crap it's beautiful! Yes GOD, Christian music is beautiful, and blessed and I want to play it, yes. Please forgive me. Hallelujah."

Believe me, that's an example of very, very mild "bad thought", and a very abbrevated prayer.

After my first flair up during a song, I get tense. I play along with recordings, so I can see exactly how much time a song has left. I tense up and tell myself, just get through this song with no more bad thoughts. No more bad thoughts. No more bad thoughts. I spend so much energy thinking about bad thoughts that they automatically come to mind. I feel so exhausted playing the Christian songs and trying to keep thoughts out of my mind.

Of course, I relax and have more fun with the secular music. And I feel guilty for it. I take some relief in knowing that GOD knows my intention and the rest is not me, it's ocd. The ocd tries to hit you where it hurts, all under the guise of protecting you. If left unstopped, it will not only take over your hobbies, it'll take your work life, and your personal life. Ocd, you can't have my hobbies. Or anything else.

More Men

Another break from ocd. Since my teens and early twenties, I've made a lot of improvements in my general attitudes towards men. I've even tried that cesspool called internet dating. As you can tell from my less than flattering use of words about it, things have not been brilliant as far as online dating goes. Sometimes, it's just been two people, me and whomever are just plain not compatible. No harm done. Other times, it's been more serious. Spiritual problems. Guys who want money from me. Let's not forget the guy who gave me ringworm.

Ringworm! The same guy was bragging(?) to me how he didn't bother washing or showering much. He just would wash his clothes, because that's what smelled. I know. Gag me. About now you might be wondering what a card carrying germ-o-phobe would be doing with some literally filthy guy like that. I suppose, in a way, I thought I could change him. And I thought I could help him to live a better life.

It wasn't just the showering issue he had trouble with. He had other problems, too. And to my surprise he didn't want to be "changed". He didn't want a better lifestyle. In addition to thinking I could "rescue" him from his, quite literally, filthy lifestyle. In addition to seeing him as my own rescue mission, my ocd can do a 180 degree turn when I really care about someone. Instead of worrying about people getting me sick, I worry about them getting sick. If they've got some germ on them, then I want it too. As I've already mentioned in the context of my earlier relationships, I tends to worry to the extent of acting like the clingy girlfriend. And I would worry about ringworm boy, too. He lives an hour away from me and would call me once a day. If I wouldn't hear from him "on time", I would start worrying about him.

Positive Change

Sometimes, but not always, change helps ocd "experiencers", as I like to call them. Or should that be us? On a trip, out of town, houseguests or any other pleasant break from the norm can prove to be a useful break from the ocd. Of course, it always comes back, but for temporary. In new surroudings I've experienced a break from ocd.

My most recent break happened in 2005 when my parents bought a duplex in a larger central Minnesota town. I made my descision to rent the lower part from them. Of course, people have made it their businesses to judge me over the years, but they're my parents. I can be there to help them if they need it. They can help me. And what can I say? They take it easy on my rent bill. I would need to pay someone anyway, and if the money has to go to someone, it may as well be them.

The move proved a wonderful experience for me, after all the hard work was done. I was in town after growing up in the country. At times I missed the quiet and beautiful scenes of the country. But I didn't miss the cliquey people of that area, and I sure didn't miss all the yardwork and creepy-crawlies that had made my ocd flake out so many times.

I had opportunities here. Real opportunities! To meet people, to make the friends I so badly desired. To learn, to take classes. So many things to do. It took a lot of adjustment.

My ocd seemed to partially take a break on me. I breathed a sigh of relaxation. It was months before symptoms started showing signs of coming back to get me. And it took a triggering event to make them come back full swing.

MRSA

It was one of my few and far inbetween dating experiences that wound up triggering my ocd again.

My date and I went to a park, a beautiful little park with a small creek running through it. We explored the paths, even the ones that were little more than a trail through the woods by the creek. We got to a smaller part of the creek. I don't know if it was my, or my date's, idea to go across. I slipped, fell on a rock and into the creek. My date seemed in no hurry, but my entire lower half was soaked and sandy. Even though I felt I'd made leaps and bounds with the ocd, I still didn't like "mystery water" on me.

So, after walking some more, I finally suggested to my date that we drop me off at my place before continuing our date. He looked at me like I was stupid before he figured it out. Oh. I suppose you're wet. Yes, Sherlock. I'm soaking wet and want to change clothes. That's what I wanted to say, but didn't.

Well, by the time we wound our way back to his car and back to my place for me to change, it must have been a quite awhile. I hurriedly changed and tried to dry off.

Awhile after that, I started getting a rash. He and I hadn't had sex, so I wasn't worried about std's. Of course, my ocd sprang into high gear. I wore myself out trying to figure out what it was. I did all kinds of research online. Of course, there were a million things it could be, but, as usual, what stuck in my head like glue was the horror stories of rare and incurable things. I asked over and over again if this was serious. My dad told me not to worry. So I would bombard my mom with my questions, panic, tears and worry over the stupid rash.

We worked up the nerve to go to the doctor. As it turned out, the harsh sand that I had been wearing around along with the bacteria in the creek gave me a very common, very treatable bacterial infection. A few pills later and I was fine. But the ocd didn't shut off that easily.

During my "exploring" of dreadful illnesses online, I had come across this dread thing called MRSA. I had gone to a music message board that I used to frequent to calm down after a particularly tirsome ocd experience earlier in the day. I went to the "general" section where message board members posted about whatever they wanted to. I saw an odd post titled "MRSA". Intrigued to know what the acronym stood for, I clicked it. I can't begin to say how many times I wished I never would have done that.

You see, I had just convinced the ocd that people didn't catch things from things that other people touched. It really helped me with a lot of the contamination theory fears, and a lot of my things that I hadn't been using because they were contaminated became clean and usable again.

I clicked the MRSA thread. Turns out, MRSA stands for a type of staph infection that can be spread through touching things that other people touched. I felt defeated.

By now I'm sure that you, the reader, can guess how this affected me. Just about every little thing became a big scary chance to get this dreadful thing. I stopped going to the chiropractor because I feared people with it went there. I washed until my hands cracked, bled and buckled. Even getting therafin wax treatments did not soften them. I cleaned, I disinfected and I showered. The same symptoms but a whole new disease to be afraid, no, wait… terrified of.

I began scrutinizing people in public for sores. Anyone with bug bites, band-aids or sunburn became suspect to me. I would hold my breath around any suspected infected person and sometimes even avoid the places that I saw them at. I would wash and scour.

No longer content to elbow doors open, I would put my purse in between my body and the door. It must've looked like a real sight, me trying to wiggle my way out of the door like that.

At this time I had my gym membership, and I enjoyed the pool in particular. You might think that a germ-o-phobe like me may not cotton (old southern term meaning take to) to swimming in a big stagnant tub of water that lots of other people have been splashing around in, but in reality, I got so that I liked swimming better than showering. The pool is as close as I can safely get to bathing in pure bleach, an ocd fantasy of mine.

Of course, the community showers proved a problem. But it wasn't a huge issue either, because I'd take hand sanitizer with me and disinfect the shower before using it. But the MRSA fear got the better of me there, too.

One day I saw a lady with her leg bundled up in a cast of some sort and up on a three wheeled cart-like contraption in the locker room getting changed. What I saw next shocked me. She took off her brace and there was a big raw and oozing open sore under there. I felt faint. I didn't know where she was going, so I hurried to the pool. I considered leaving, but the pool was much closer. I wanted the quickest way to get away from leg-sore lady. I started my water aerobics class. And all of a sudden, who should come wheeling in but... that's right... leg-sore woman. I kept a paranoid eye on her as she wheeled her way into the pool room. "Maybe", I thought to myself, "maybe she's going to the other pool". She moved like a turtle, but who could blame her, with her leg in a cast. I watched in slow motion as she lowered herself into the same pool I was in. I stared blankly at everyone else in the water aerobics class as she took a lane to do some laps. I might as well stay in now. I tried telling myself that the chlorine would take care of whatever she had. I tried telling myself that the other people in the water aerobics class were taking the same risk I was by staying in the pool. I tried and I tried. I went in the hot tub later.

Leg-sore lady finally left and went back to the locker room. I stayed in the hot tub a long time, hoping that the "clean" hot tub would cleanse me. I knew I'd have to get out though and face the locker room. I had to handle the door that she did, and I had a slight chance of using the same shower she did.

Another lady went in the locker room before me. I waited to use her shower. My line of reasoning told me that the other woman was a buffer, incase leg-sore woman had used that particular shower, too.

I used my hand sanitizer, but somehow it didn't feel strong enough. I got home and showered, washed, cleaned and sanitized. But then I did something that gave me great faith.

Who knows how much more severe the washings would have been if I hadn't prayed. I prayed to GOD to not let me get the sores. And then I told myself that GOD is all powerful and in control. I was able to relax a little.

However, pretty soon going to the gym, even though I was not using the pool, became a chore. I could no longer feel safe or clean there and the cleaning rituals and contaminated items when I got home were so stressful. I boycotted going to the gym, all the while paying my membership fee each month. This lasted for a long time. I went many months without going back there.

Yet another way the ocd stole a hobby from me, but I am happy to say I got it back. Today, though I still sanitize shower stalls, I can be able to enjoy the pool.

Scrupulosity

I think back on my earliest ocd symptom - washing Mary and Joseph. It seems some illogically logical that I should have developed scrupulosity. Scrupulosity is the religious or moral form of ocd. Sometimes it manifests as a fear of wronging people, or sometimes it takes on religious themes. I read of it in an ocd self-help book. While I was reading accounts of people with scrupulosity, I thought to myself, "What an easy fear to get over. GOD knows about everything, including ocd. These people should stop tormenting themselves and realize that GOD knows they don't mean anything bad". Of course, I knew that ocd symptoms could change over time. I just didn't think that I , myself, would ever develop scrupulosity. I was aware of it. I was even thinking rationally about it. But boom! All of a sudden there it was.

I was in a long distance relationship at the time. I would have to wait a long time to meet the man I was in contact with. I really liked him. Then, all of a sudden, I would worry. I would worry about this man, whom we can call Joe, like I did about my pen-pal of years and years ago, Bisq. The imagination was very similar, and since this man in particular lived in Europe at the time, I knew he walked a lot of places. I worried about violence.

My mind would make up strange scenerios. Some man would walk up behind Joe and strike him in the head. Take his money and run. Joe would be at a bank and there would be a robbery. He'd be taken hostage. And who could let me know what happened to him when I hadn't heard from him?

As with Bisq, our main way of keeping in touch was computer. When I didn't hear from him for several days, I would even Google search his names to see if he was in the headlines, to see if something bad had happened to him. Of course, nothing did, but the bad stories my mind was making up didn't go away.

I began to pray for him. At first it was quite soothing. I would basically ask GOD to keep Bisq safe. And the I would feel so wonderful about it. It was in GOD'S hands now. But then the thoughts of harm coming to my dear Joe would send me over the edge again. I would pray again. The prayers got longer. And then the bad thoughts while I was praying started. As I would be praying, unwanted and horrid thoughts would come into my head. I hate thinking them, I much more hate saying or writing them, but to give you, the reader, an idea of the torment, it would be things like "Dear Father GOD you're a ********. " (Insert a horrid word there). I didn't mean to think that. I'd flake out. I'd feel my face turn red and my heart rate go up. Where did that miserable thought come from. I didn't mean it. "Dear Father GOD", I would start praying again. "Please, please forgive me. I didn't mean that. GOD you are an AWESOME GOD…" and then I would have to ask whatever I wanted all over again, after asking for forgiveness. Of course, it wasn't that simple. The thoughts would come again, and again and again. I would beg forgiveness and pray an opposing thought like the example above, but then it would come again. Sometimes I wouldn't even be finished asking for forgiveness for my dreadful thoughts.

There were other variations on that theme, too. Even after I would get all done with a prayer, which I have a very special way of closing a prayer thought would come. I end prayers with the word "Hallelujah". Sometimes a common swear word would creep into my mind directly after a prayer. I'd finish my prayer with "Hallelujah"… and then my next thought would be "crap!". No, no, no! It's as though the thought had contaminated my whole prayer that I just got done with. As with playing the Christian music, I would tense up. I knew I had to get through the prayer with no mistakes or else I would be stuck praying again. To prevent the prayer from being contaminated by a bad word at the end, I now concluded most prayers with "Hallelujah and only good things, too. YOU, not ocd." Then, even if I thought the vilest of four-letter words after it, I had inserted the buffer of "only good things…"

Sometimes I would have so many different bad thoughts while praying I would get confused. I knew I had to "undo" them by praying something opposite.

Another example that is still unpleasant but not too painful to write about is this prayer "Dear Father GOD", and I would be struggling for the rest of my prayer. Struggling for the rest of my true, honest prayer. I felt anxiety creeping up the back of my neck. "Dear Father GOD… shit to you!" I was abhored! I had meant to have a heartfelt conversation with my Heavenly Father and here I was thinking these terrifying thoughts that I didn't mean to begin with. It was like something had taken hold of me. So, to undo that one I would start over "Dear Father GOD… please forgive me. Blessings and flower petals to you." I don't know why I needed to add the words "flower petals"… but I think I needed something to visualize while I was praying.

Sometimes I didn't even need to think the bad words within the context of my prayer. Sometimes all I needed was to visualize things. These things too would leak out of my head while I was praying. The vision of a pile of dog poo, for example. I would re-start my prayer, this time visualizing something nice, like flowers or a cross. I wore myself out praying. And so little of it was the actual conversation with GOD that I wanted. The most of it was bad thoughts, terror and praying for forgivness and to undo the horrid thoughts. And, oh boy, did those thoughts ever stack up. Trust me, these were just the easy ones to write about.

The thing with Joe didn't last. He got here, we met, but we weren't right together. But that didn't mean the scrupulosity left. If anything, the scrupulosity got worse.

Now I didn't have to even be praying and a bad thought like the ones I mentioned above would float into my head. While I was doing anything. Schoolwork. Showering. Getting dressed. Getting ready for class. At class. Writing e-mails. On the phone. Talking to people. Shopping. Eating. Anything you can imagine. I had to devise ways to pray with out people noticing.

So far, an effective one has been to stare at something behind the person's head as I repeat my prayer for forgiveness.

Sometimes I've gotten stuck in what I like to call "prayer cycles" for long spances of time. When I'm exhausted, sometimes all I can do is to pray for GOD to forgive me, and to help me with the tormenting ocd.

Sometimes my mind pictures people while I pray. Then I feel the extreme need to ask GOD to forgive me. I'm not praying to whoever I visualized. I'm praying to GOD and I know that HE knows it. It's just so scary not to apologize.

My scrupulosity doesn't always take on a spiritual theme. Sometimes I worry about having lied to people. It's a quality to be honest, but when you're honest to the point of being flat out boring... it's something else.

Here's an example conversation I might have with a friend.

Me: ... "I haven't been too busy, I went to Sarah's coffee shop the other day..."

Friend: " I'm cutting back on coffee, they say it makes you gain weight. Well who knows right, ..."

All the while my friend would be talking, my mind would be elsewhere, still obsessing. Did I go to Sarah's coffee shop, or to the big chain coffee shop? I don't remember... maybe I lied. My brain would still be struggling with this and then I would re-join the conversaton and some later point ...

Friend : (me, having missed a large section of conversation due to worrying about being honest) ... "So I told Erica, no way!"

Me: *stammer* "So, uh... you... uh... know the coffee shop I went to?"

Friend: *pause* " ...Yeah..."

Me: "Well, I'm thinking that was really that big chain coffee shop right off of First Street. (quieter) ...I can't be for sure though..."

Friend: *extended pause*," ... Oh... yeah... "

Me: (feeling sheepish) "So, uh, what now about your friend Erica? What did she want you to do?"

Friend: "She didn't want me to do anything, she wanted my advice on her new boyfriend."

Me: "Oh... I see..."

These types of exchanges leave me feeling quite upset. I don't mean to appear unconcerned about other people or their lives. But when I try to calm the fear of lying, my ocd tells me that I wouldn't want others to lie to me, and that I might be asking for that to happen if I'm not accurate with what I say. I've even called people back (you know who you are) to correct some little trivial detail.

Another thing that does not win you any social medals is not speaking in absolutes. But sometimes it just slips, leaving me in an awkward situation.

Me: "I always go to the Basics store in the mall... pause... well, you know, almost always. No wait. I shop at Essentials, too. And oh yeah! I like Bookies, too. Yeah, that's on the other end of town though. So, yeah. I almost always shop at Basics. You know, when I'm at the mall anyways. Sometimes. But I don't exclusivley shop there. Or at the mall...", voice growing quieter,... "uhm, just when I'm there... and stuff..."

Again I don't wish to seem so critical. I have no clue how this type of thing sounds to other people. I must sound like I'm disturbed. Or stupid. Or like I'm hung up on myself. And this plays back into the sometimes crippling fear that what I've said sounds stupid or has offended people.

Joe Chen

Remember the man from the previous story? The one that helped my scrupulosity get started? I wanted to include this story here, because I feel it will be helpful to others, even if it doesn't directly tie into ocd. Meeting Mr. Chen, as we could call him, helped change my attitude, even if our relationship didn't work out.

I had mostly given up on meeting anyone off the internet, but I had left a few profiles up anyway. One day I got a message from Joe. It was a different sort of message. It wasn't the misspelled masterpieces that I got that read something like, "hi wuz up? want to chat" or the somewhat more vulgar but still common "got any nude pics? Send them 2 me". It was an actual letter. And better than that, it had details about Joe himself, and questions about me as a person and not the size of my breasts. It seemed all too good. He was intelligent and funny.

We moved from writing letters, to voice/video chatting online. We saw each other in real time, so no surprises for either of us when we would finally meet, and we had wonderful time.

We talked about all manner of things. Intellectual to trivial. He said he thought we were soulmates and couldn't wait to meet me. I couldn't have been happier. I was glowing. He was nice, smart and good looking. And he actually took care of his appearance. He was serious, but he knew how to be funny, too. And though money made no difference to me, I do admit that I did find comfort that he was successful in his line of work as a computer geek. If he was successful, he wouldn't be interested in me because he thought he could get something from me. I'd had men hint around before. Bisq, for example. And two previous boyfriends. One kept questioning, "How much did *this* cost?" "How much did *that* cost?" "I bet that was expensive, wasn't it?", and statements like that. Pretty obvious.

The other one, in describing a previous relationship, told me that he had gotten used to a certain lifestyle because his girlfriend was well paid.

Well, Joe was doing fine on his own and when I Googled him, the websites proved that he had many degrees in the fields he'd told me about. A weight lifted off my shoulders. I didn't need to worry about him being after any imagined money I might have. You would have thought that I would have learned something from the whole incidence with Bisq. But by now, that was years and years ago.

Well, I did get to meet Joe. But something wasn't right. He wouldn't make eye contact with me. His body language was way off. Way, way off. It wasn't that he wasn't trying to molest me, it was that he would face almost opposite from me. He seemed tense. I thought he was just nervous. But there it was, the next couple of times I met him, too. The funny blank stare. The funny hugs that felt like I was hugging a close male relative, rather than my so called soul mate.

After he moved here from Europe, I generally heard from him very seldom. I assumed he was busy settling in and getting used to work. His work was very demanding. It was about all he would talk about. He went from interesting to a work-drone. I scraped for conversation. About the only thing that excited him anymore was work related. So that's what we'd talk about. He said he'd call. And he didn't. I'd leave it go, and go and go. But it was starting to drive me insane, or at least more insane than I already was.

After the various odd types I'd dated, here was someone I was actually into and all of a sudden he was shutting me out. When I did finally get him on the phone I would hint around, trying to get him to say what made him into a different person from Europe to here. He would just mumble something about being busy. Then I point blank asked him why he was acting differently. All he could do was mumble something about me being an hour's drive away. I still remember him saying how we'd have to hang out all day to make it worth while. I felt shocked. People drive an hour to work. An hour to shop. An hour to see family and friends. I didn't get why it was a big deal, and besides he knew that I'd be an hour away before he ever met me.

To be honest, I don't know what his real issue was. But whatever the case, we didn't work out and I was again stunned that people didn't say what they meant, particularly when I'm such a stickler for saying what you mean.

So, right about now you may be wondering why I decided to tell you this in my book about ocd. Because, the point that I want you, dear reader, to walk away with is the fact that even situations that appear negative can be positive.

As things began disintegrating with Joe, I made some comparisons. True, I was pretty upset with him. But really, why was he able to pursue a successful future and travel the world and accomplish things that he wanted? My answer, I decided, was that he thought something of himself. He was intelligent.

But I, and doubtless many others, had the same intellectual abilites as he does. He is nothing special. I wasn't dissatisfied with my life at that point. But I was in a rut. Doing the same things, not taking many chances. Not saying "yes" to a whole lot of things. I made my first big choice directly after we split.

I went to college for the first time at age twenty six. I hadn't gone before because of a few reasons, like I didn't know what I would take. I didn't feel moved towards anything really. But one thing was I didn't think I was worth the investment. Joe proved to me that I was. And now, one and a half years into my college experience, I'm enjoying it.

Yes, the ocd has made things difficult at times. For instance, even choosing the school I wanted to go to. I already knew that I don't like crowds, so sitting in a class of 300 or more wasn't for me. I already knew that I feel generally insecure around people my age or younger. I couldn't picture myself getting along with some 18 year old valley girl wannabees, not that's what all 18 year olds are. So I chose a private night school. Less people to confuse me, and less germs to spread to me and contaminate my stuff. Grown-ups as classmates for the most part. Not that I have anything against young 'uns, but I already feel strange enough without my Generation Y brain having to learn Generation Z speak, the whole new language what the young 'uns speak, with a whole different culture to go along with it.

Also class discussion proved difficult. I'd think that something I wanted to ask or bring up was stupid. I'd be silent. Someone else would bring it up and the instructors usually thought it was brilliant.

I'd obsess about getting papers to feel "right" enough to turn in. Nothing feels right enough, and it's very seldom that I feel confident in turning things in. Sometimes I'm happily amazed when the teachers grade it high.

The college was the big thing that I said "yes" to. But I said "yes" to other things as well. Sometimes small things. Yes, I would meet a friend for coffee even though all of my rituals weren't done. Yes, I would be more open and not judge everything I said. Yes, I would open up, at least a little around trusted people. Yes, I would try new things. And then something came along that I didn't think I would do.

National Conference and Nightline

The ocd support group that my parents and I participate in went to the Obsessive Compulsive Foundation's national conference in 2009. We were asked if anyone wanted to talk to the media. After my experiment in saying "yes" to opportunities, I thought to myself, "There's something you don't hear every day", and said "sure". It wasn't as easy as I made it sound. There was a lot of doubt in doing it. Ocd is something I've tried to hide from people for years because I, and probably a lot of ocd experiencers, realize that the obsessions are illogical, and the actions to get rid of the obsessions are equally as irrational. Sometimes I felt downright stupid trying to explain myself. What seemed to be natural in my head was so very difficult to explain outloud.

After talking to a few wonderful people working for the OCF, I was told that the TV show, ABC's "Nightline", was interested in talking to me. The producer called me. I had a half and half chance that the producer would be female, easier for me to talk to from my previous examples. Of course, it turns out that my producer for the segment was male. I instantly felt threatened, simply because of his gender. As we talked, I felt a little better. When we met, I realized that he was attractive.

I temporaily reverted to my old way of thinking about men in general, and men that I find attractive in particular. I tensed up. My mind figured that he was probably smug and would be, in any moment, laughing at me. This time the man knew some of my secrets. Something to really laugh about, not just my physical appearance.

I approached him a little more vigorously than I would have normally, as I was doing my "confident act". Within minutes my mind was put at ease. He seemed very nice and easy going. He seemed caring and poking fun of me wasn't on his to-do list. I was amazed, talking to him was easy enough. The same with the camera man.

I slept very little that night and got up early enough to read my chapter a day in the Bible before they came to film me early in the morning. And then I had two of *them* in my room alone with me. Two men in my room. I was certainly outnumbered now. Somewhere in the back of my mind, I wondered if this was going to be a rape scenerio. I would like to say that they did nothing to make me think they were going to assault me. They both behaved in a very professional manner. It was only my paranoid mind making up stories again. I brushed it aside. I was nervous enough, but once they started filming, it was easy enough.

After I met my interviewer, John Donvan, I was again pleasantly surprised. He was so nice and easy going. Talking on camera felt like a conversation instead of an interrogation, like I had imagined it might be.

Back at the conference, I was acting as room monitor for two out of three days, so, for some of the time, I had very little choices on what sessions to attend. But the surprising thing to me was that even if a session sounded like it didn't apply to me, I learned something from every session.

I also learned to let confrontations with people go. One man was confused about what session he was at. I normally speak really quietly, even when I'm talking to people. This time I did a loud whisper. One lady came up to me, in the middle of what I was saying, insisting that I should leave the room. My whispering to the man had distracted her and if I had to keep talking to him I should leave the room. I think people don't realize that the room monitors are, for the most part, volunteers and that we don't think of everything. It didn't occur to me to leave my "post" at the back of the room.

She kept talking, making me feel stupid. I tried assuring her that I was just answering the man's question, and she kept repeating herself. The man walked off. I told her that the man was out of the room now. She kept talking. I let her. I felt alittle upset and even angry at this woman.

But then I realized, this is a conference for people who have ocd. Who knows, my whispering could have set off some ocd ritual in her. It seems unlikely, but then again, I have had some pretty unlikely rituals, too, like flushing aliens out of my eyes. She could have really been having a tough time listening. Telling off the room monitor, who thought she had the right to actually whisper answers to questions to people, maybe was a huge boost for her self confidence. Maybe it provided her with crucial exposure therapy. I can't begin to guess about it or about her. But guess what? I disappointed someone, and it's alright. I can't please everyone.

I went to a scrupulosity support group. It was so exciting to see others with different versions of what I had, but I had a hard time talking about it. I still do. Scrupulosity is painfully difficult to talk about.

The big event of the night was Dr. Jonathon Grayson's virtual camping trip. I had second guessed going on it several times, since I knew it was exposure and response prevention. But Steve, my producer from Nightline, said that they had wanted to. Now I felt I would be letting people down if I didn't.

By the time Dr. Grayson got done with his introductory speech, I felt a lot better about it. I'm happy Dr.Grayson addressed a lot of fears about ocd.

He made people who were afriad of knives handle them. He had us kick tires in a parking lot. He asked hoarders to throw away papers. But I knew what was coming.

He asked if anyone had hand sanitizer. I hesitated. Of course, I did. That's how I manage in the germ filled world. It keeps me from running to the bathroom to scrub everytime I feel "germy" or otherwise not right. And on this trip I knew there wouldn't be any chance to wash.

After a brief pep-talk with Dr.Grayson and a dear, sweet little girl, I handed over my newly filled handsanitizer, which he promptly emptied and then threw away. There I was. Totally without sanitizer. I froze. My stunned look must have been evident. The camera man came over and pointed his camera at me. Steve asked me what I was thinking. I tried to say outloud what I just wrote. I managed to stammer something about the doctor taking away my safety net and knowing that he was going to have us touch stuff. We walked on.

There were a couple of homeless guys we were supposed to give change to. That was enough for me. Handling money and giving it to a homeless person who probably didn't have easy access to a shower or other hygenic supplies. Then he did something totally unexpected and kissed my hand. I about flipped. The man had missing teeth and some kind of funky mottled or lumpy complexion. I must have looked as germy as I felt. He said something to me. I don't know what anymore, but I felt bad. I didn't want to hurt his feelings or anything. But that's the way my ocd rolls! It freaks me out to look at people with spots or sores or whatever, because I imagine that it could be contagious. I definitely, under normal circumstances, don't let them kiss me.

The night was not over for germ-o-phobes yet. We made our way down an alley towards a garbage dumpster. Dr. Grayson had people who weren't afraid of germs reach in the dumpster, effectivly contaminating themselves. I cringed for them. Dr.Grayson made an awesome speech. I'll include it here.

"Think about how much it has stolen from you, how many times you've been humiliated because of your OCD," said the doctor. "How many times there's something you wanted to go to and you didn't get to go, how many times you wanted to be in a relationship and your OCD stood in the way. And if you have parents or loved ones, how many times you tortured them, you made them do your rituals. You're beginning to try and take your life back."

We did a group hug. "Contaminated" people and "clean" people. They were contaminating us as Grayson talked. I blanked out. But as I reread it here, now I see why I was crying while he spoke.

Think of all the things ocd has stolen and how you've hurt family and friends. Dear reader, if you have ocd, please take a minute now to think about that, because it hit me like a hammer. This beast in my head was not only taking over my life, it was hurting people who I love. I fought tears. I could feel the light from the camera above me. I don't like openly displaying my emotions like that.

Two people hopped into the dumpster. I really hoped that they weren't going to have us all do that. We didn't, but it was difficult. Germ-o-phobes got in a line to have dumpster people rub garbage on them. I cringed. The camera man, now perched happily on top of the dumpster, was motioning me forward. I almost laughed. I wanted to motion to him to get in line. I went forward. I remember cringing inside my own skin as dumpster person #1 shook my hand, and dumpster person # 2 rubbed a plastic bag in my hair. My hair is notoriously hard to clean. I held my hands away from me until I could wash.

I caught up to Jackie from Teak Media. As we walked, she said she was really touched about participating in such an event. I was amazed. Here was someone who didn't have to be here experiencing the fear and nonsensical rituals that go along with ocd. So I asked her why. And she said something about how it was great to see real people being brave. She was on the verge of tears and so was I. I didn't answer her. I was avoiding crying on camera, and besides, I knew I couldn't fix my eye makeup until I washed my hands.

The other challenge of the night was to rub your hands on a public toilet seat (something I avoid using) and eating a tic-tac without washing. Disgusting. I knew from the dumpster experience I wasn't up for it.

Steve wanted to talk a little more on camera after the camping trip. I told him I needed a minute to compose myself. I washed, and then I fought tears even more. I don't know what hit me so hard right then and there. Dr. Grayson's speech. My insecurities were flooding back. I composed myself somewhat. I talked to them. I thought for sure I was rambling incoherently. Surprisingly, Steve, whom I had thought was intimidating at first, seemed like he actually cared. I wanted a hug right at that moment. Not a hot-and-bothered, press-your-body-into-mine hug… just a regular hug, hug. I didn't dare. It was an odd sensation. Usually I'm not "huggy".

I hung out with my good friend later. My mind was a whirlwind. I slept somewhat better that night after a long hot and decontaminating shower.

The second day was amazing. My mind felt over loaded from the events of the previous day. I slept in and took time out to enjoy a swim. I went to a session and to the social event, the banquet. And then I hung out in the lobby. I was enjoying this. There was always someone to talk to, and no one with an attitude. We probably all in some way shared something. Interesting people. It was all so exciting.

The next day was a half day, and people were packing up. What a whirlwind. It inspired me to go on mini-adventures when I got home and to try even more new things. I got over a lot of the germ fears. I even went swimming at a beach, something I hadn't done for years. Go to the park? I don't know where it is! Normally I'd have said no, but when a friend asked me, yes! Why not? Let's go! Summer flew by.

When January rolled around, Nightline came back, the same people I'd met before. They were really professional, but this time was more strange.

At the conference it felt right, the setting wasn't at home. This time they were in my home. I found it more difficult to talk and far more difficult to to show the cameraman my morning rituals for a comparison. The interview was alright. I hoped I was coherent.

As the time dragged on for it to be aired, I grew nervous. What if I had said something stupid? I probably looked fat and ugly anyway. I sighed. I wrote the now patient producer, Steve, some e-mails. I was a little nervous. How do you present something as crazy as what I was doing and not make me seem like I was off my rocker?

But I was quite pleased with how it was handled. Informative and carefully handled. They actually did use that part where Steve talked to me after the dumpster diving camping trip. I thought I was babbling incoherently, but I made a clear point.

I was surprised. I received some wonderfully kind e-mails that confirmed what I wanted to do with my Nightline appearance. It's much my same goal with this book. I want to enlighten people. I want to help get rid of stigma. I want families and friends of people with ocd to know what the ocd experiencer is going through, and I want people with ocd to not feel so alone.

I remember watching a man with ocd named "Rob" on national TV when I was newly diagnosed. And it felt good, not that he had ocd, but that I wasn't alone.

Party Activities

At your next get-together, why do the same old things like serve hors'douveres and talk around the fondue, when you could experience the mind of ocd with some of Frederique's ocd rituals.

Foot-Toilet Flush

See how much dexteriety you really have with your feet and find out how high you can raise your leg in this game. Simply flush the toilet with your feet. Not as easy as it sounds. For added fun, play with foot-cabinet open or foot-drawer open. Think of it as a variant on the limbo. See how many things you can open or operate without knocking stuff down or falling over.

Toilet Paper Contamination

Tired of the bathroom being empty when you need to use it? Instruct guests to scrutinize the toilet paper. Sure it's going to get dirty, but is it clean enough to touch you there, to begin with? Better check, and double check to be sure. Throw away any odd bits and go through rolls. Fun for the entire family.

Clock-Blink-Stare

Here's a game that you don't even need a bathroom for. Make up your own bad numbers and the observe your digital clocks. When the clock hits a "bad" number, refuse to do anything, and move as little as possible. Please note the possibility of as much as ten minutes in this fashion, when double digit numbers are used.

Play Doctor

Pick any slightly odd spot on your anatomy. This can include things like freckles and bug bites. Rub, poke and otherwise agravate the area. Do detailed internet searchs for vague descriptions "slightly red patch on skin". Pick the most negative possible diagnosis. Worry for hours. To do this one justice, wait until late at night, right before you go to bed.

Phone Trivia Tag

Remember your "bad" numbers from the clock game and apply those to phone numbers that you dial. When you simply must call a phone number with "bad" numbers in it, call a "good" number. Dial 1-800 - first. Don't worry, they can't charge you until you give them a drecit card number and besides, all you need to do is to dial the number to "un-do" the bad number you called.

Silverware Bingo Bonanza

Closely scrutinize your silverware. Examine in detail any mystery spots. Waterspots you say? How do you know it isn't, oh, say tuberculosis? What are you, a doctor or something? Get new silverware, pronto! For added challenges, do this at a restaurant and figure out how to sell the waitress the story that it really is dirty after you've asked for thirty or so pairs of silverware. Silverware Bonanza Bingo. The game that's as much "fun" (if you can call it that) at home as it is in public.

Of course I don't want anyone to start doing ocd rituals. And if you already have ocd, especially avoid my ideas. At times, one must take ocd lightly. Don't be afraid to laugh at it, as long as it's laughing at the ocd and not you as a person. If you do not have ocd, you might even want to try some of the rituals or imagine yourself doing them. I think it would give a new prespective to it incase you were curious about how difficult/frustrating/time consuming this ilk really is. If you're supporting something ocd, you can use humor to your advantage, but it would be wise to err on the side of caution. At one point in time, I was especially sensitive about all of the rituals I'm writing about. They were tormenting. Now after years have gone by, in most cases, I can see them for what they are. False alarms.

If you know someone with ocd, chances are they've got older rituals that are not a huge issue for them, they might be at the stage where they can laugh at some of them. Let them dictate which ocd rituals are laughable.

Guilt Trip Frequent Flyer Miles

The "beauty" of this one is that in can be done anywhere and at anytime. Let you mind travel back to any recent conversations you had. Pick them apart for accuracy. Find a discrepency and ponder what kind of lie it was and if someone acted on your information, what it could have caused. This is similar to an exercise in cause and effect.

Thinking Your Way Out
Of a Wet Paper Sack

Sometimes your own thoughts can be your worst enemy. I was reading something on appreciating the randomness of thought. Anyone with ocd can probably tell you all about the randomness of thought. It would be interesting to be able to think, just think and not be worried what your anxious mind is going to spring on you next.

Some of the most difficult to explain ocd rituals are the thought rituals. I had them as well. The thought was something bad happening to me or someone I love. I don't like to be more graphic than that. Then the ritual, to go along with it was to re-do the action that I had been doing whenever I had the thought, while thinking an opposite "good" thought.

Thoughts happen all the time, so this manifestation of ocd has led me into doing and re-doing a great number of things. Getting out of bed. Getting into bed. Everything in between. Turning on the shower, TV, radio, computer. Changing TV channels, picking up the phone, doing housework, writing, reading, cooking, eating, drinking, walking, rewalking.

True, if I had a "bad" thought and sometimes, had even managed to ignore it, it would only rear its ugly head later and come back twice as strong. I'd have to redo it.

The most difficult ones to redo were the ones that involved retracing steps. Sometimes I'd have to go outside walk to my car, touch the car, and walk back. This one in particular was to undo the thought of someone getting in a car accident.

But it didn't stop there. Anything on the above list and just about anything you can imagine I'd have to do and redo until I finally thought the right thought.

Attract More Flies
With ... Vinegar?

Inspired by my experiences with the dating world, I thought I'd share with you something I wrote around Valentine's day of 2010.

"I'm so tired of the singles scene, so I'm making this fake profile. I can't bear to be this sarcastic on my real one."

"Hi! I'm 19 years old and have modeled for 16 magazines, including some popular men's magazines. Teehee, I guess I'm popular because I'm blonde, 6 feet tall and weigh 130 pounds. I know the 130 sounds sort of fat, but 30 of it is the silicon in my size EEE breasts."

"I like riding around on four wheelers, sports of all types, being active, fishing, hunting, trapping and rock climbing, all while wearing high heels, and keeping my hair and makeup looking immaculate."

"But you know what I like even better than that? Taking orders from you!! Oh, please invite all your friends over to my place and have me wait on you and them hand and foot. Oh yes, also please degrade me in front of all your friends and talk about me like I'm an object. That makes me so hot!"

"So, who I'm looking for: well certainly someone who wants to help me spend my money. You know I have too much of the stuff anyway, and I'm really hoping that you are way older than me and have a beer gut and shower every other week. You should dress in whatever makes you comfortable, but I really like the grubby sweat-clothes look. It's so hot. I mean, it's totally right up there with the t-shirt with holes and sweat stains look."

pause

"So ... does that sound entirely hilarious? It should! But I think it's what most men on here are looking for. A porn star look alike, who acts like one of the guys unless she's between the sheets. In the meantime, some of these same guys pay little attention to their own appearance or even basic hygienic skills."

"So now, for the real me. "

"I'm not 19 (add a 9 to that number). I'm not blonde, and no, I'm not a super model. If you're about to click away after reading that, stop and ask yourself: are you a super model or George Clooney look alike? I didn't think so. I'm not a wafer thin model... and somehow all my weight hasn't managed to settle in my boobs.

That said, I'm not ugly or huge-as-a-whale either. I'm average.

I'm not wealthy. I'm a college student.

I'm Christian.

I like what I like including taking walks in parks, photography and music, to name a few things."

"Please don't contact me if you're:

"Out for a one night stand. (This has happened to me) ."

"Going to decide that a 20 minute drive is too far for you to bother seeing me. (This has happened to me. Let's be real here, a lot of people drive 20 minutes to go shopping, go to work, go to school…)."

"A liar. (This has happened to me)."

"Married to your work. (This has happened to me)."

"Married to your wife."

"Want me to listen patiently to all your troubles with your ex-girl friend. Are you interested in me, or in her? (This has happened to me)."

"Going to treat me like a therapist (hire one!) (This has happened to me)."

"Going to treat me like a housekeeper or babysitter (Hire one!)."

"Going to treat me like a prostitute (Hire…. Oh wait…. Don't hire one!)."

"Going to lead me on and then, after I wonder why you won't do something simple like hug me, turn out to be gay? I mean why even bother with me in the first place? (This has happened to me)."

"Going to grope me in a fashion that feels like you're an eight-armed octopus. Being held is nice; feeling like I'm wrestling with an octopus – not so sexy. (This has happened to me)."

"Still reading?"

"That said, I'm nowhere near as bitter as I sound, and this wasn't intended to be caustic. It's meant to be a caricature of the online dating world as I've come to know it. Some of the women online are almost doubtlessly as odd as some of the men. "

"Well, if you are not any of the above things, can hold an intelligent conversation for more than 3 minutes and are somewhat hygienic *and polite, contact me. Your picture gets mine, but remember I don't mind if you're not a Jonas brother, so please don't mind that I'm not Britney Spears or whoever it is you like these days. "*

I actually did post this online. Now I had written heartfelt personal ads before, detailing me as a person and trying to work in charm and wit... and I would get oh, I don't know, maybe a handful of replies. I wrote this, posted it and within the first day of it being online, I got over twenty replies from this sarcastic masterpiece. It might go to show that it really is best to speak your mind. Surprisingly enough people are difficult to offend when you're not being outright insensitive.

Commonalities

As I have been writing, I notice that there are some common ground in the fears. For example, the pregnancy, fire and AIDS fear all included the fear of judgment of others. The germ, alien and soul stealing camera fears all have the fear of comething incorrectable, unfixable or otherwise untreatable. Even the fear of the common cold, it wasn't just the common cold I was scared of, it was going deaf, or staying "stuck" in a cold-like state that frightened me.

My ocd experiences, no matter what the specific fear is, usually include first, the lack of trust in myself. Internal questions like "But did I check it good enough?", "Is it really off?", "Am I really clean?" even though I know that I have indeed checked, cleaned or otherwise did the the action.

The second thing that the ocd uses against me with any of the fears is the overactive imagination. The imagery of the dreaded event happening in minute detail. It's the gas for the ocd which is like a mental fire.

It makes it difficult to be rational at times. When there is a concern or an issue I find myself wondering, "Is this ocd? Or me? Would a normal person be thinking this?" And I have no internal answer because I have nothing to compare "normal" thoughts with "ocd" thoughts. Even with non-worrisome thoughts, I tend to find myself wondering "If I didn't have ocd, would I look at things this way?" I suppose the answer is to live and let live. And to somehow try to turn this brain-drain called ocd into something positive. That's what I hope to accomplish with this book.

And no matter if you, the reader are dealing with ocd or something else entirely, just look at me, with all of my ridiculous fears and rituals. If I can turn ocd into something brilliant in my life, then you can too! I challenge you, reader, you to make something positive out of a drawback in your own life.

Writing Myself Out of My Own Life

How do you write yourself out of your own life? It's a valid question. And with ocd it can be surprisingly easy.

This ritual ties into scrupulosity. If I think a negative thought, something the ocd tells me is blasphemous while I'm thinking about something I'm about to do during the day, I have felt the need to not do the action I was going to do, in order to deflect GOD'S anger. Deep down I do know that my thoughts are just that. They are only thoughts. GOD knows my true intention and GOD knows my heart. My mind drifts back to what I first thought after reading about scrupulosity. That GOD knows everything, including about ocd. But the fear feels so real.

If you don't have ocd and are reading this book the thing I'd most like you to take away from it is that people with ocd usually realize that they're acting illogically, but the fear of the what if is just too great. The fear feels real. That's the motivator, the fear. And so it goes.

I have written myself out of so many things. I've written myself out of going shopping, wrapping gifts, cooking, eating a great deal of things, going online, and contacting people to name a few things. I've put off projects I've wanted to do. And it's not that I don't want to do these things. But the fear of doing them and thinking I've offended GOD by it is too great.

Many times these things are some of the things I've most wanted to do. The ocd kicks you where it hurts. My default time has been one day, though a few things were a year at a time. One day turns into two days, and from there it can drag on. Sometimes I actually get dis-interested in the activity before the ocd will allow me to regain right to doing it.

It's a cruel and vicious game the ocd plays. On the days where the ocd had written me out of particularly a lot of things I want to do, about all I can do is realize what it is and tell myself that if I keep it up, it'll write me out of everything that's important in life.

I visualize the ocd as an evil twin, out living my life for me while I live my reduced lifestyle. I realize that it can't continue like this and sometimes, just sometimes I get my days back.

We Are Family

The ocd has impacted my family situation, too. I would like thank my parents for all of their patience with me.

To my dad who also has ocd, thank you so much for putting up with my question asking and for the offer of help anytime, even at the middle of the night. Thanks for answering things, even when they might have incited your own ocd. Thanks for being proud of me even though I haven't always been conventionally successful, and thanks for telling me that you love me and for all of your input on my extracurricular homeschool activities like woodworking, mechanics and driving. Thanks dad for always being there for me and never abandoning me.

To my mom I would like to say thanks for putting up with my whining, and repetitive questions. Thanks for reassuring me, even though I keep asking and even though my efforts to explain my fears likely made no sense what-so-ever. Thanks for being so happy for me and for telling me that you love me, even not exclusively, but even when I'm in the midst of an irrational whirlwind of mucky mucky mental illness. Thanks mom for continuing to listen to my imagined (?) fears and wrong-doings from others, and being my reality check.

I would like to tell families of someone with ocd that your support is so crucial to someone with ocd. I would also like to add that I know it's difficult for you too. It's hard to see someone you love tormented, and it's equally as hard to get dragged into it yourself. You may be in the middle of enjoying life and yet your loved one, seemingly insensitivley whines about this or that imagined fear. It's hard, I know. Please get your loved one professional help if possible. Please seek help for yourselves. You need to know how to help your loved one while not get dragged into their world of mental illness yourself.

Also, please don't help us. I would like to apologize to both of my parents for all the times I roped them into my ocd rituals. Though it made it easier for me at the time, your loved one needs to go through the discomfort. You could try being with them while they do the difficult thing for moral support, but please, unless your loved one is on the brink of a breakdown and simply cannot handle it. That's what I've found most helpful. A mental health professional may have more ideas.

Likewise, please don't pressure or get angry at the person with ocd. Keep in mind that no matter how agitating their symptoms are, they probably don't mean to upset you. The ocd is doing good enough at upsetting them. They probably don't even want to do whatever the ritual is, but the anxiety caused by not doing the ritual is too painful.

When you need to approach them, please remember that it's a far better approach to gently remind them that you, as a person without ocd, would not do the ritual or have those thoughts. Remind them that the ocd is doing this and they don't need to live in torment.

If you have ocd, you can share "war" stories. You can tell them that you don't mean to boss them around, but that you see the worry taking over their life and as a loved one you don't want that for them. Please remind them to work on their problem when they can handle it. If a person with ocd feels pressured or like they have to quit something, it'll only make the pressure worse, and with more stress come more ocd symptoms. It's hard, as not only someone with ocd, but a family member, I know for sure that it's hard to have it and hard to put up with it in others as their obsessions and compulsions start to become your own. But please know your support is ever so important and vital to your loved one and that gentle encouragment goes a long way.

Ocd experiencers, please realize that your mental state rubs off on your family. If you do ask for reassurance, please try to limit your questioning. Trust your loved ones to not lead you wrong. Please know that your torment becomes theirs as well, only it makes even less sense to them because it's your torment, not theirs.

Please take time to talk about other non ocd things with them, and if you ask for advice please consider it, at least for a little bit before making up your mind. Even when it seems like they're nagging at you, please know it's only because they can see your torment and want to help you and that this is the only way they know how.

Words of Help, or, What Has Worked For Me

I'm not a mental health professional by any means, but I have the overwhelming desire to share what has worked for me with my own ocd experiences. I hope it provides some help to those of you reading this book.

Washing and Contamination

One of the first things I that I can remember actually helping with the washing and contamination fears was grouping tasks together. For example, if I had to:

...wash my hands before playing with the cat, wash my hands after playing with the cat, put the clothes in the laundry, wash my hands, turn on the radio, wash my hands and then eat lunch...

I might start by cutting out one washing, say in between playing with the cat and putting clothes in the laundry. I'd keep grouping tasks that were, in my mind, dirty in bunches like that, and wait to wash until something important, like eating a meal or cooking, was happening.

Also, dear washers, please take care of your hands. When they crack and bleed, it only makes you more suseptible to infections. There are a number of wonderful lotions out there that won't irritate rough hands. A place to look would be your local medical supply store. Butter also works without burning too much. Don't be afraid to treat yourself to a therafin wax treatment for your hands at a salon. Don't worry, salons are required to maintain a certain level of cleanliness. The treatment will help to heal your angry dry hands and may provide you with more motivation to not wash so often.

I can remember the first time I got my hands treated. "Do these belong to me?" I remember asking myself. So soft and smooth.

Washers, I ask you to remember a time when you didn't have this washing compulsion. Did anything bad happen to you? Did you get any of the illnesses that you fear? Did you get sick more than the average person? If you did, do you think, honestly, that it was your lack of cleanliness that made it happen?

Quietly observe someone that you trust. Someone who isn't a "washer". Do they get sick often? Do they get the things you're afraid of? Likely not. And one thing is probably for sure, they probably have a much easier time enjoying life than you do.

Trust in your body's immune system to take care of diseases if you would happen to be exposed. Remember some of the people wth the strongest immune systems get exposed to a lot of different illnesses.

Relying on GOD has helped me a lot. Saying a prayer for comfort and protection against diseases has helped me a lot.

And keep in mind, that in a way, the ocd causes the thing you're afraid of. For example, are you really scared of getting sick? Think hard. If you do, you might find, like I did, that it's not so much getting sick that you're afraid of. You're afraid of feeling icky, and of being exhausted. You're afraid of being sick and not enjoying yourself or special times. And isn't that about how you feel when the ocd comes on, full force? Don't you feel icky and exhausted and certainly not able to fully enjoy yourself? That's what I found.

Thought Rituals

Thought rituals are difficult to talk about and hard to explain. If your thought rituals are mostly to keep others safe, please think about what hurts them the most. Your distance from your loved ones hurts, and it hurts a lot. Your rituals can keep you from being close to the ones you care so much and, in essence, you are actually hurting the ones that you're trying to protect.

If you're doing thought rituals to keep yourself safe, think of it this way … if you think to yourself " I am now 20 feet tall, I am now 20 feet tall, I am now 20 feet tall…", that no matter how long and how hard you say it, you will not be 20 feet tall by the time you stop. The same goes for your "bad" thoughts, and the same goes for your "good" thoughts. The only thing that you are really insuring is that your mind stays occupied with ocd thoughts, while not living up to your true potential to be who you're meant to be.

General

Remember, that you have ocd, or you could say, sticky brain. Sticky brain wants you to feel "just right" all the time, but at a huge expense to you. It costs you your time, your relationships with others, your self esteem, and your energy. All of these are things that money cannot buy. It robs you of your precious resources and can interfere with your happiness and wellbeing.

Now for all of those things that sticky brain wants to "protect you" from, what kind of guardian charges that kind of price? The kind of the guardian that is your worst enemy. Even though it seems to protect you, even though it may seem like your friend at times, trying to keep you out of harms way, it's harming you all along. In a way it is the worst kind of enemy anyone could have. It's the kind of enemy that stabs you in the back.

Maybe you've had ocd for some time now, and have experienced symptoms that changed over time, like I have. Maybe you are waiting for an easier obsession to come along. Something easier and not quite as scary to work on. In my example, it was the alien and camera fear. I don't like to tell it to you, but that's not a smart idea. Work on fighting the ocd now, because it doesn't get easier. Sure some of your symptoms may be less difficult to work on than others, but the ocd doesn't give up that easily. In my experience it'll keep coming to get you. You can get over one fear only to find yourself trapped by some other fear that makes the previous manifestation of ocd seem tame the next minute. It's an ongoing effort, and waiting to work on your ocd only seems to keep you imprisoned by it longer.

There are many therapies available for ocd, if at all possible please seek professional help for yours, and if professional help isn't a posibility for you, please check out some of the wonderful self help books that are available.

Consider telling people who don't know that you have ocd about your struggles. I know. It's scary. You have no clue how they'll react. But in my experience, no one has had anything negative to say to me about my having it. In fact, you might just be surprised at how many of your friends or family know someone else who has ocd, or you might find some fellow ocd experiencers to share your tales with.

Sharing also gives you a wider support base of people, ready to help you if you need it. And you might even get the added bonus of them trusting you more and sharing more with you. What a wonderful feeling. Sharing your ocd experiences can deepen and strengthen friendships. And if, for some odd reason someone should be less than kind to you, please know it takes a very small minded person to think poorly of someone who has something they can't help. Would that person pick on someone for having diabetes? Likely not. You can't "help" having ocd anymore than you could diabetes. But you can work on controlling your symptoms, just like a diabetic can take insulin and diet and exercise.

Should someone be small minded enough to treat you any differently, that person probably has some sort of issue that they're insecure about, too. Would you really want that kind of person as a friend, and especially a trusted friend?

Support groups can also be a wonderful experience. You can get to know others with the same thing you have. You might not have the same symptoms, but you all share the irrational fears. It can be self esteem boosting to see others with ocd beat some of their fears. It can be a place where you can talk about it and know that almost everyone else knows where you're coming from. Wonderful friendships can happen.

Scrupulosity

I've heard the word scrupulosity as pertaining to a wide variety of ocd symptoms. Painfully enough, this can even include thoughts of offending GOD.

In this case, it helps so much to remember that GOD knows about your ocd, and HE knows who you are underneath the brain chemical disorder. I don't think that GOD wants limited prayers... sometimes limited to chanting GOD please forgive me... over and over again. Scrupulosity doesn't bring you closer to GOD, it takes you further away. When you cut yourself out of your own life, or pray the same phrases over and over again it's like your prayer is tainted with ocd. At least in my humble opinion. Why give GOD your ocd?

As for worrying about wronging people, do your best to be responsible and then let other people take the responsibility. People occasionally became resentful when you "hover", and it's ironic because you are likely only trying to look out for the best of whomever, but when you don't trust them enough to be responsible for their part of whatever your shared situation is, you invite them to resent you for treating them like they don't know what to do.

There are many other ways scrupulosity can manifest, these are the two I have experienced, and therefore they are the two ways I can give advice on.

No matter how your scrupulosity manifests and no matter how scary it is, you are one ahead of it already. You know that you have ocd. If you react to your irrational thoughts, it's almost like you believe them, which, since they trouble you so greatly, you obviously don't. If your thoughts have to do with GOD, He, too, knows what thoughts are yours, and what thoughts are your ocd trying to torment you to pull you away from what is truly important and special to you.

Whether or not you "write yourself out of your own life" like I do, in one way or another the ocd, no matter what the manifestation, ocd works to pull us away from our lives in many different ways. From the professional who is too busy worrying about whether the door is locked to truly listen at meetings, to the parent who can't enjoy their own children out of fear of what kinds of germs they dragged home, or the people who need to buy seven pairs of just about everything to prevent running out, when their house is already full, the examples go on and on, but the similarity is that ocd is taking these people and even, arguably, everyone who suffers from it away from their own lives.

A point in time comes when one must decide to live their own life, even when the ocd is screaming at them "You might get hurt", "You might hurt others", or "What if", whatever the ocd tells that person to keep them under its thumb.

To that I say, "What if I let you, ocd keep running my life? I'll always be nervous and not really present for the things that really matter to me. You can make me anxious ocd, but you cannot run my life." I hope that affirmation helps any ocd sufferer like it has helped me.

A Purpose

Maybe you are like me. You feel adrift at times. You wonder why you're here and what you should be doing. You want to make a difference. If you have ocd yourself, you may wonder why you have it. Perhaps you reflect on all the things you could with the time you've spent ritualizing and worrying, not to mention all the time you've spent concocting strange stories inside your head that keep you worried. To that I say, not only to the ocd experiencer but to everyone, let's take our negatives and turn them into positives!

For me, an example of this is when and how I decided to go back to school. That's in an earlier chapter. But a point that may hit home more so is what I decided about my ocd. If I have to have this tormenting brain-draining illness, then I'm going to get something good out of it for all the time, effort and energy that it's cost me.

I've been more vocal about it. This started in the local ocd support group, and continued when I was asked if I was interested in being on ABC's Nightline and was interviewed by two local newspapers.

But if you ask me, I think the ultimate expression of my turning ocd into something positive is this book. I sincerely hope that by my writing about things, often humiliating and sometimes embarrassing, that I can reach others. I wish to make those who have it feel less alone. I want to comfort families and friends. It's not your fault and you can't fix it, for those of us who experience it. I want to write in a way that is entertaining, even sometimes laughing at the ocd, of course. Not the people who have it. I think humor is a healthy way to deal with ocd, when it's appropriate, of course. I want to interest people in what it is, and in what it isn't.

In fact, one of my biggest gripes about a popular TV show that features a lead character with ocd, is that they also portray him as a selfish, greedy and uncaring jerk some of the time. While some people with ocd may be of this type, it's not a symptom of ocd. In fact, we with ocd often get ourselves into trouble because we care too much for others.

I want to show people that this can be tormenting. And I want to show people that it can get better and share what has helped me. What a way to use ocd to my advantage. I hope that you, the reader, take whatever difficulty you might have and use it to your own advantage as well.

Volunteering, as I have also found, is a great way to find a feeling of purpose. There are so many places searching for volunteers that it isn't hard to find one that fits what a person might be looking for. If one doesn't work out for you, keep trying and I'm sure you'll find something rewarding. I have had my ocd push me out of volunteering at nursing homes and the local veteran's hospital. In those instances, it has been the fear of germs that got to me. The showers and cleanings afterwards got so bad and stressful that I would dread them even before I set off for the volunteer gig. However, I have found another opportunity to volunteer at a local organization that helps people with disabilities, and I find it so enjoyable that I don't even consider it "volunteering".

Another wonderful way to take power from anxiety is by immersing oneself in your passion. Mine is art. I enjoy photography, theater, jewelry crafting, needle art, painting, dancing and playing instruments. Maybe yours is art. Or maybe it's politics, reading, the outdoors, hunting, camping, fishing or something else entirely. Delve into it. Take classes or join a club or group. Go on outings you never thought you would. Expand your horizons, and start saying "yes" to things, and I think you'll be pleasantly surprised where life takes you. I know that has been my experience.

Say "Hello" to Your
New Compulsion

After working hard with my therapist on my two main symptoms, I noticed an odd thought one day as I was driving. That thought was, "Have you turned the stove off?." It hit me like a physical sensation that could best be described as someone throwing a bucket of ice water on me. I was instantly uptight and scared. The same lack of trusting my own senses and memory came back, just like they had been in my earlier fear of not shutting the cd player off. I managed to keep driving.

I noticed it once after that, and the thought came on twice as strong. I almost turned around. A wave of anxiety hit me. I even remembered wiping off the stove; none of the burners were hot. But that wasn't enough for my ocd. Maybe the stove was just on simmer. Maybe I was remembering another day that I'd turned the stove off and not this day. I bit my lip and kept driving. I knew in the back of my mind that if I dared to give in to the anxiety and turn around, even just this once that… that was it. I'd be toast. I might as well just say "hi" to my newest compulsion: checking the stove. Could I risk the house burning down? Probably not. But I knew I couldn't risk turning my life over to ocd again for a whole new compulsion, either. And guess what? The stove was off and the house was still standing when I got home.

What I Still Deal With

As much as I would like to tell you that I'm entirely free from ocd, fear and anxiety... that would not be the truth. I've noticed during my experiences with ocd, right when I start making progress with one particular manifestation of ocd, and start feeling better, then boom! There's another new symptom (or sometimes even an old symptom) to deal with.

In my teens, I would tell myself that I would wait for an easier-to-conquer fear to roll around. I thought that once I was sucessful in beating my current fear I would be over ocd. Was I ever wrong about that.

Most recently, I'm still dealing with germ fear. I still wash and sanitize more than your average person. I get more sensitive about it in certain circumstances. For example, when I have a cut or scratch, it becomes all too easy for me to imagine some bad microbes getting in there and turning into something bad.

My main symptom right now is scrupulosity. It's so easy to rationalize it out on paper, but so very difficult when your mind has you on the brink of tears because you are stuck thinking things that terrify you, things that you certainly don't want in your head, but there they are, time and time again. It's so very difficult to not give in to the urge to pray, or repeat information over and over again.

But at the core of it, it's the same as any other manifestation of ocd, it's the same old "what if" story that ocd uses to keep its sufferers under its thumb, sometimes for the most of their lives. That scares me, too. Who do I want living my life for me? The ocd? Or me, myself? How would I feel if I could see the ocd in the form of an evil twin. An evil twin who torments me and keeps my captive in a dungeon, while it goes out and lives my life for me.

I still write myself out of my own life. That is incredibly frustrating to say the least. Some days I'm left with not being able to do too much. Some weeks I'm left with not being able to do too much. I'm trying to not let that turn into months, years and decades, and I know that if I don't stop it now, that it will only get more difficult and try to write me out of more of my life.

I still fight with the fear of numbers, too. So at least you can be sure that I'm concluding this book on the right number of pages.

My Mom's Story

"My name is Vicki and I don't have ocd, but I live with two people that do. I am their 24/7 support group." I've used this introduction many times at our local support group, so much so that I wonder if the members are getting tired of hearing me say it! Anyway, here's the brief version of my story about our family and our daughter Frederique's problem with obsessive compulsive disorder.

As a parent, you want the best for your child. You're always on the lookout for things that may harm them, and you're there to kiss away the boo-boo's – whether they're real bumps and scrapes or the occasional imaginery "monster" under the bed.

As a mom with "no-ocd", I was not at all prepared nor did I understand the "monster" that was in my daughter's head, namely obsessive compulsive disorder. When it first appeared at about age three or four, it was so cute when Frederique would go to the drawer where the Mary and Joseph statuettes were stored and she'd secret off to the bathroom, close the door and repeatedly wash them each time we visited the relatives. They say hind sight is 20/20. In retrospect, if only we had known at that young age what lay ahead for our daughter, we would have done things differently.

Who knows – there were probably a few other "oddities" and "cute" little things that she did over the years that went unnoticed, but were in actuality ocd symptoms. After reading what my daughter has written, I am heart-sick to find out that there were so many things that she secretly suffered with. I just want to hug her close and cry.

Then came the dreadful pre-teen and teenage years. Ah, all those hormonal changes that were happening, along with the budding of ocd, which we didn't know was coming about at the time.

I couldn't figure out why all of a sudden she believed that she caught a cold from a pen pal letter and why she was asking me hundreds of times in a day, day after day, when would she feel better, would she die from this cold, when would the cold be done with – you get the picture. She had had colds before and recovered from them. What was so different about this one? This went on for days until I couldn't take it any more and would bark back with some answer, hoping that this one would be the right answer and I could FINALLY get through to her. I knew her ears were working. I knew she was hearing me, but why wasn't she *listening* to me and believing what I said? It made me feel like I wasn't much of a mother. I couldn't make a difference. Nothing I said was getting through to her. WHY? I couldn't kiss away this boo-boo. I felt helpless.

When the hand washing began, once again I tried to make a difference. Scolding, nagging. begging, arguing – nothing seemed to work to help my daughter not to wash her hands bloody. It just seemed to make things worse when I tried to help. I'm her mother, I'd think. I'm supposed to make it all better. What was I going to do? Will she ever have nice soft hands again that some young man would love to hold? I was very frustrated and felt ever so helpless. I'd gladly have taken this torment for her.

Another thing that lingered was chronically being late to be somewhere, leave the house, etc. This was in the days before she learned to drive, and her dad and I were the chauffeurs. What was taking her so long? I had told her earlier in the day that we would be leaving at a set time. Why couldn't she be on time, especially when she knew hours before at what time we would be leaving? What was she doing? "Are you ready yet?" This caused a lot of anxiety and sore feelings for both of us and Frederique as well, as were about to leave for what was supposed to be a fun time out. How would she ever be able to make it on her own? We finally discovered that it was those horrid rituals that were taking so much of her time and energy.

We used to tell her we'd leave without her, and to prove the point, one time we did just that. This time she was particularly behind schedule, and so her dad and I got in the car and drove off. We never lost sight of her in the rear view mirror of the car, though. She got really scared and knew we meant it, and she was better about being ready to leave on time for quite a period of time. This didn't last though, as the ocd got worse.

It finally came to a time when my husband and I knew we had to intervene and find someone who could tell us why our daughter was doing all these strange and what seemed like harmful things to herself. Finally we found a psychologist who was able to diagnose what was wrong with our precious child. Obsessive compulsive disorder – what's that? We bought books and started to research the disorder. While learning more about our daughter's condition, we also discovered that her father, grandfather and great grandmother also had the same condition. It was in their genetics – that explained a lot.

They weren't crazy – they had a brain chemical disorder. It was comforting to find that out.

Having been married to my husband for a quarter of a century, it was a shock to both of us to discover that my husband had it too. I never had any clue that he was checking and counting repeatedly like he did. He kept it well hidden, as did Frederique with some of her compulsions.

Time and counseling sessions went on, and nothing was seeming to improve. We found a psychiatrist who seemed to understand what was going on. She thought it was worth a try to prescribe some luvox – the only drug approved by the FDA for ocd. Maybe this would be the light at the of the tunnel. It was worth a try. It seemed to work at first, but then as the ocd symptoms faded, so did our once vibrant daughter. She was too tired to do the compulsions, but also didn't pay attention to important things either, like her check book and credit card balances. While driving, she would go on red and stop on green. This was getting too scary and hazardous for us, so after about a year on the drug, we insisted that she stop taking it. Although the drug seemed to help with the ocd, it was stealing our daughter. Getting off the luvox was not in the doctor's plan, and she refused to assist us. We remembered how Frederique had slowly increased while take the drug, and so we just reversed the process. Success – our daughter was finally back, but so was the ocd.

More years went by, and so did our daughter's life. There were so many things she declined because of the "monster" in her head. I remember one time trying to reason with her and the ocd by telling her to picture the disease like we used to see in a well known commercial – the devil on one should with his pitchfork and horns, and an angel on the the other with wings and a halo. The ocd, of course, was the man in the red suit, and the angel ultimately would win the battle. Sometimes it worked, sometimes it didn't.

At times, the ocd was worse; at times it was better. In the meantime, my husband faced his ocd fears head on and was able to keep it under control for about 8 years.

Eventually we moved to a new area with hopes that the move would be a help to conquer the ocd. It did help for a short time being in a new house, but the rituals slowly crept back into our lives. We searched around and found a support group just for ocd. Frederique was quiet at the meetings for a period of time. My husband and I both found it relieving to know there were others like them, and we hoped that she would open up and get some of this "monster" off her mind. Indeed, she did eventually start to talk about it and the rest is history, with Frederique doing newspaper interviews and being featured on an ABC Nightline segment.

A common saying in our home is that, "You know it's ocd. Think about it and you'll be able to give it up when you're ready." We feel that knowledge about ocd is so important for everyone involved – know what it is you're dealing with, both for the "experiencer" and the "no-ocd'er".

As time goes on, I feel less helpless with the realization that this is a brain chemical disorder. It's important for me and my husband and daughter to be able share with others through our support group the it is possible to have a "noocd" life!

My "no-ocd" Conclusions

- I can understand and comprehend what I read and hear about ocd, but I don't know what it "feels" like.
- Knowledge about ocd is important, both for the sufferer and for their families and friends.

- There are plenty of books and websites with information about ocd available.
- The brain can change when these fears are faced and dealt with, but it's not easy. *"You will remain the same until the pain of remaining the same is greater than the pain of change." Anonymous*
- Scolding, nagging, arguing about the obsession or compulsion doesn't help anything. It only creates more anxiety which makes the ocd worse.
- Don't be an enabler by letting the person with ocd make you do their compulsions. It just fuels the ocd fire. Set limits and stand your ground – after all, *you* don't have ocd.
- Talking to others about ocd is important therapy both for the sufferer and family members. It can be an uplifing experience. Seek out support groups, a good counselor/therapist (one who specializes in anxiety disorders and/or ocd). Even chat rooms and web groups are available on the internet. You can't and don't have to go through this alone.
- Eventually the ocd symptoms will dwindle and the sufferer will tire of doing them. BE PATIENT – they will know when it's time to give it up.
- Learn to recognize some ocd symptoms. If you notice them, talk with your loved one about it and find out from them how you can best help.
- It seems to me that a lot of these ocd compulsions become habits quickly if they're not caught early on. A favorite quote of mine is: *"We first make our habits, and then our habits make us." John Dryden*
- Remember that ocd is a brain chemical disorder and that your loved one is not crazy. The brain is an organ just like any other organ, and is subject to disorders and diseases as well.
- People with "no-ocd", as well as those who have it, have thousands of random thoughts in a day, but our brain

processes them as just that, a random thought, without letting us linger on them or consider that they maybe some sort of bad thing that would have us do some ritual to "make it all better". *People are not their thoughts – it brings them all kinds of sadness.* "Peaceful Warrior"

With enough skills in place to handle those "ocd moments", life can be a blessing rather than a curse. Hang in there and strive for a "no-ocd" life!

"Come to edge, he said. They said, We are afraid. Come to edge, he said. They came. He pushed them, And they flew ..." Guillaume Apollinaire

The following story was written by my mom as an assignment that was done in our support group. The purpose of the story was to name the ocd and write as if she were the ocd speaking.

S-T-A-N-D I-N

S—Second Guessing

T—Terrified

A—Anxious

N—Negative

D—Depressed

I—Incoherent

N—Not Present

Hi! You can call me "Stand In". That's the name Frederique's Mom has given to me. I am really Frederique's Obsessive Compulsive Disorder. According to Mom and Dad, that's how they see me. I am real and I don't like it that they are on to me. I will fight as hard as I can to keep my title of "Stand In" for their daughter, Frederique.

I can't believe how good I am! I have stolen so much from Frederique and her family. Sometimes I just suck the joy out of life for all of them! It makes me grow stronger each time I can be Frederique's "Stand In". I don't want to quit, but Mom and Dad do not like me at all and want me to leave so they can have their "real" daughter back.

Let me explain how I work.

"S" is for Second Guessing. I steal Frederique's true first impressions and intuitions so that she is doubtful about everything.

"T" is for Terrified. I rejoice each time she is so scared of things that others call normal. I make her so afraid that she has to do some ridiculous thing just to get some temporary peace.

"A" is for Anxious. Frederique is never calm about anything and I love it.

"N" is for Negative. Oh happy day! I make sure Frederique is not positive about any aspect of her life. I have lowered her self-esteem to the bottom of the pit. I have every negative thing in her life stick in her mind and push out all of the good things life has to offer.

"D" is for Depressed. I am joyful for this one because when Frederique is low, I am high. Frederique's bad moods bring down her whole family, but it elates me. Another success!

"I" is for Incoherent. Frederique can't think straight and concentrate and gets easily confused when I am in control.

"N" is for Not Present. When I am in full control of Frederique, she is so bothered by the things I make her think that are not true that I have her undivided attention. This makes for a confused Frederique and her life does not go smoothly.

All in all, I think I have done my job as Frederique's "Stand In" well, and I will continue to thrive as long as Frederique and Mom and Dad leave me alone. I really hate it when Frederique learns more about me and can try to fight some of my attacks. What I hate worse is when Mom and Dad come on the scene and get involved in Frederique's fight against me. They are the strong ones and I can't stand them. I have tried my best to take over Dad's life as well, but he figured out how to successfully fight me and win, so I must try harder to completely ruin Frederique's life. Mom and Dad want their "real" daughter back. I will fight them whenever I can, but I think that they may eventually win and I will lose.

My Dad's Story

Thinking back in time to when Frederique was about three years old, Vicki and I noticed some really cute things that Frederique would do, like the washing over and over again of Mary and Joseph. It seemed to us that Frederique was so loving to the little statues that she just couldn't get enough time in washing them. We didn't understand yet that there was something far more to Frederique's overwhelming washing of the statues than what we were seeing.

Frederique was a very polite, kind and caring child. She made us very happy. She was, at such an early age, so very conscious of colors, shapes, the order in which things were, and Frederique was always aware not to offend others around her. She would always be on guard as to how to be considerate to others, so we were not having a difficult time in raising her. She was an intelligent child, always so quick to catch on to things, which later, in part, proved to be a downfall concerning the ocd. Those nasty ocd compulsion habits would quickly form a groove in her brain and, at times, would prove to be hard to get rid of.

Many years before I knew that there was a label and name to those "odd quirk" type things that I did, the ocd was just common to me. Over the years, I've come to realize that I was not even thinking about ocd or the bad habits that I was doing. They were just there. The compulsions easily become bad habits, and I would do them without even thinking about them.

I always had similar habits to Frederique, yet I never thought of ocd as a problem, for we all were only too concerned with everyday life.

My wife had no idea that I was doing these odd behaviors, as they were so much a part of me that I just did them. She wasn't aware that I was counting while praying, checking the door lock or light switch, or any of the other odd things I might have done at the time. I don't know if I could say that I hid them from her – they were just there.

I was always very afraid that my family might get hurt, so I couldn't do things good enough. Everything I did had to be overly perfect. I wanted Frederique to be as perfect as possible, and she caught on to this concept very quickly. It was natural for her. I knew that we were all supportive of each other, and to this very day, we all still are.

By the time that we all knew that there was a name to this behavior of Frederique's, we figured out that this name also pertained to my actions as well. We all studied books and began getting a lot better understanding of why Frederique and I were going through the repetitive things that we were. I recognized myself in many of the statements about ocd in the books, as well as seeing what it was that Frederique and I had. It helped me a lot to know that it had a name and that acutally, not just us, but a lot of other people had this condition called ocd.

When I think back to my childhood, I must have been about seven or eight years old when I can first remember having some worries and repetitive behaviors, although at the time, I didn't know what it was. It was just a part of me.

When I would get a cold, for instance, I would repeatedly quiz my mother about it. Would this stuffy nose kill me? Would I get better? How long will it be before I get better? Questions like that all day long. My mother would answer me, but toward the end of the day, she was running out of patience after hearing my questions all day long. Finally, she would snap back a response in a very stern voice. "Listen, Buster," she would say. "People are going to think you are buggy. You just stop that now. You will be all right." By the tone of her voice and the look on her face, I knew that there must have been something about what I was doing or saying that was wrong. She wasn't upset by my cold. If there would have been something wrong with me, she would have said that we would go to the doctor the next day. By that , I knew that IT MUST BE ME, but I couldn't figure out why or how it was me.

In about 1998, I had an incident which took place in which I got so MAD that I had a sort of war with myself. One day when I was outside at one of our outbuildings, I was doing my usual lengthy, time consuming ritual of checking the lock enough times so that I would be able to walk away from the shed feeling safe. I would pull on the padlock, to make sure it was locked, in sequences of "lucky" numbers, so many times that, on this day, I felt I was at war with myself. I said to myself in an extremely aggressive manner, "NO WAY! I am NOT going to continue this bizarre counting ritual!" I told myself, "STOP IT! The shed and house will be all right if I don't go through this ritual of counting … 48, 52,… times." I said, "Leave it alone until tomorrow and check it and see. The shed won't burn down and no one will break into it." "This will be my proof today (on that particular day) that in the morning when I come out to check the padlock, everything will be all right." This would prove to me that all of this excessive checking and all of my other repetitive behaviors (even my scrupulosity which was going on at the time) was not real. I needed to be able to stop all of this excessive and repetitive behavior that I'd grown to hate about myself.

The next morning came and I went outside. The shed and padlock were just fine. I went into a huge victory outburst, saying to myself, "This does it! No more of this needless and absolutely ridiculous time consuming ritualization of ocd behavior." I felt TREMENDOUS over this victory, and in fact, I had no more symptoms of ocd from that day on, which included the scrupulosity, where I would pray nearly all day long and in certain numbers of prayers. The checking and counting of door locks, light switches, etc., were gone as well.

So many years went by that I forgot all about my previous ocd behavior, because all of it was done and over. This victory lasted for about the next eight years.

I've told this story many times at our support group. People tell me that they get a feeling of hopefulness when they hear that I really conquered the ocd for a long period of time. That makes me feel good to know that my experience can help others.

After the time we moved to a different location in 2005, we had searched out a support group, and life began getting easier to see that many other people also suffered from this disorder.

About eight years went by, and all of a sudden, with my severe back pain, I was put into the hospital. Upon being released and coming home and being given strong pain medication, I now found on the first day being home that I had my ocd symptoms back, perhaps even stronger than they ever had been prior to this. I had no idea how or why this got started up on me again.

I have discovered that each time I have a bad pain flair up or get sick, the ocd comes back.

It's been a struggle since then, but I have been able to identify it as ocd, and with the help of family, books and the support group, I can work with finding ways of keeping it under control as much as possible.

These days, with all that I and we have gone through with ocd, I find that there are things that I can suggest to Frederique and my wife that will help with some of the ocd symptoms that Frederique and I are faced with from time to time. This makes me feel very good that I am able to help Frederique out with her ocd in some ways.

I understand that through life, ocd will be ongoing, both with our study of it and with both Frederique's and my symptoms. Due to my lenghty eight victory over ocd once before, I would like to think that there may sometime be a technique or something included in a therapy that would allow much longer victories over ocd.

Also working with groups to educate others about ocd is very fulfilling and rewarding. I look forward to doing this as well.

Dad's Shed Victory Story

Since my childhood, one of the most trying and aggravating times with obsessive compulsive disorder turned out to be a fantastic success.

At this point in my life, I had no idea that the turmoil I was going through of feeling that our shed would either be burned down or broken into by thieves was, in fact, ocd. I would have these feelings everyday, sometimes several times a day.

I would use items from the shed. It was an old shed where you could see through small knot holes in the wood into the shed. Upon leaving the shed, I would check the padlocks in number sequence, which were to me, lucky or unlucky, like even numbers were lucky, odd numbers were unlucky. I couldn't stop with a mere 2 or 4 or 6 as I jerked on the padlocks to make sure that they were locked. I would stand there jerking so that the numbers would go as high as 112 or more.

Along with doing this, I would constantly be praying to God for forgiveness of any and all sins that I MAY have committed. The prayers also had to be gone over time and time again in an even number sequence, or I would feel that either God punish me or us, or that something terrible would happen to the shed, our home or us personally if I didn't pray or check the right amount of times.

These rituals could take a combined time in the day of at least and hour more. I had absolutely no idea that what I was doing was nothing other than a bit of an UNUSUAL habit.

This had been going on in my life for years, along with checking other things and praying excessively throughout the day in other places as well.

The fear that I had of not doing these things was extremely overwhelming if I would not do them.

One day when I went to the shed to get a tool out, it took just a brief moment to grab my tool and start to lock the shed up again. As I was at the door leaving, I realized that I was again going to be getting "held up" at the door for a very long period of time going through the rituals.

Something that day happened to me that is even yet fully hard to understand the intensity of what took place. I got FURIOUS! I felt I was being ATTACKED by something I couldn't even get my hands on. In my younger years, I had been in plenty of fights where I could physically put my hands on the person I was fighting. I couldn't put my hands on what I was being attacked by. Yet I knew my life was being destroyed a day at a time with these terribly powerful compulsions. My only temporary bit of freedom came from giving in to the rituals of praying, counting, checking, jerking and twisting on the padlocks to make sure EVERY time that the doors would be locked solid and the lights were turned off as well.

All of these procedures for me to be able to leave the shed were very repetitive and getting worse practically day by day.

I was not only furious at the unseen enemy, but I felt that the only freedom I might EVER get was that I had to, then and there, that day, challenge it. I thought to myself, "I'm not going to go through all of these repetitions again today. If the shed gets broken into or burns down today, then tomorrow morning when I come out to check the shed, I will know if I have been going through all of these repetitions for nothing." It all would have been foolishness on my part of the cruelest and most intense torture that I would have been doing to myself for years. So, the next morning if the shed was is good shape with no problems, I then would know that this unseen enemy had, in my life, been just stomped to pieces and these rituals never needed to be done again.

Upon leaving the shed, I looked back one more time at the padlocks after checking them that day. I paused as I looked at them and thought, "Well, tomorrow morning will be the answer to this great war I've been having."

That day I felt a sort of unusual easienss, like if I had just confronted a powerful enemy and it seemed as though the enemy may be on the verge of crumbling and falling apart.

With it being the next morning, I had many ritualistic prayers in the house, but not quite as lengthy as other mornings. I was anxious to see if something had happened to the shed. After breakfast, I headed directly out to the shed, as I hadn't let my wife or daughter know what battle I had been going through.

I got to the shed, turned the corner, noticed that the shed had not been on fire, doors weren't kicked open and the padlocks were still locked! So, I unlocked the doors as I was thinking, "THIS IS IT! I HAVE DESTROYED THIS HORRIBLE ENEMY. NO MORE OF THIS CRAP (all of those nasty rituals) FOR ME!" It was over in my life. The enemy was defeated. "IT'S DONE!" I was happier than if I had just defeated the worst criminal I could possibly have come upon. Right then and there I realized that all of those compulsions in my daily life, as what I now know to be ocd, were completely obliterated. The enemy was destroyed. I REALIZED THAT I WOULD NOT HAVE TO GO THROUGH ANY MORE OF THESE HORRIBLE PROBLEMS THAT I HAD BEEN LIVING. IT WAS OVER!

I successfully stopped all of the ocd rituals from that morning and for the next eight years. Over the next few days and weeks, I had even forgotten all of the years of those miserable repetitions and agony since I was a pre-teen.

During the years that followed, I completely lost all traces of any ocd. It was like a distant dream from the past. I had no desire to do any of it. IT WAS GONE!

I have shared this story many times at our local support group and at other venues where members from our support group have spoken about ocd. It seems to be a favorite story for many of our members and others who have heard it. It was a very powerful experience for me and I'm glad that I can share it with others. They tell me it gives them hope that they too can fight this ugly monster and be done with it. That makes me happy.

Contact

Writing this book has been a wonderfully insightful and healing process for me. If you desire to contact me with any feedback, feel welcome to use the contact information below.

E-mail: nocdbook@gmail.com

Book's website: http://www.nocd.info

Frederique's personal website: http://www.fvldesigns.com

Resources

- The International OCD Foundation
  http://www.ocfoundation.org

A huge, searchable database of help and support.

- If you enjoyed this book, you might also enjoy "The Boy Who Couldn't Stop Washing" by John B. True tale of an ocd "experiencer" turned therapist.

- The Central Minnesota OCD Support Group
  http://www.ocdsupportgroup.com
  ocdsupportgroupcmn@gmail.com